"NO, N-O-E, NO"
THE CICERO RIOT STORY

H. M. Edwards

Copyright © 2011 H. M. Edwards

All rights reserved.

ISBN: 0615597343
ISBN-13: 9780615597348

DEDICATION

I would like to thank God for all of his blessings, especially for my family. I would like to thank each of them for their contributions in the past and in the writing of this book with details that I never knew or refreshing my aging memory from the oldest to the youngest.

CONTENTS

	Forward	1
1	My Summer Vacations	3
2	Do As I Say	20
3	Back In A Day	31
4	Who Has A Secret	46
5	Fiction or Non-Fiction	52
6	Facts, Nothing But Facts	56
7	Business As Usual	65
8	Can't Do Anything Right	82
9	"They Did It; I Saw Them"	89
10	"It Wasn't Us" - The Aftermath	106
11	"I'm Still Standing" - Perspective	133
	Vitae	172
	References	178
	Necrology	197
	Author	199

FORWARD

- 60 Years Ago - One Family was Accused of Starting Chicago's Second Worst Race Riot -

Attorney George C. Adams and Charles S. Edwards, Realtor, were in the business of buying and selling property. They bought the wrong property from the wrong person in the wrong town. Almost five thousand watched as the riot reached its peak. The lawsuits and aftermath left one family member dead and others hurt, physically, psychologically, and financially for decades to come.

The white owner of the burned building in Cicero claimed that my family was, "A group of colored incendiaries on the prowl for a chance to light a fuse." (The Camille De Rose Story, 1953)

Time Magazine wrote on Oct. 10, 1951:

'SEQUELS Worse than the Cicero Riots,' Edmund Burke said that he did not know how to indict a whole people; but last week the Cook County, ILL. Grand jury found a way of misusing the power of indictment to disgrace a whole metropolis.

The grand jury investigated the riots at Cicero, an all-white town, where Harvey E. Clark, a Negro, was prevented from moving into an apartment that he had rented (TIME, July 23). Not one of the 126 persons arrested for rioting was indicted. Instead, the grand jury indicted George C. Adams, a Negro, who is part owner of the building where Clark leased a home; Charles Edwards, a Negro rental agent who handled the deal, and George N. Leighton, a respected Negro lawyer who acted as attorney for Clark and for the National Association for the Advancement of Colored People after the riots started ...The three Negroes, Leighton, Edwards and Adams, are accused of 'conspiracy to damage property.' The grand jury seems to think that it is wrong to rent an apartment in Cicero to a Negro, wrong to defend his rights, but O.K. to burn his furniture and chase him out of town. (unk.)

THIS IS THEIR FAMILY SAGA, AND THE TRUE STORY BEHIND THE CICERO RIOT.

Cicero Crowds (Adams, G.)

Chapter One
"My Summer Vacations"

In my pubescent years as a middle child, it was chocolate laxative given to you under the guise of candy, pepper blown towards you as you were reading from the Bible in church, being tripped and cutting one's chin, or being forgotten to be walked home from the bus stop. Growing-up brought its challenges, especially in a large family, in the fifties and sixties in Chicago, and in a country that had little tolerance for anyone of color. Who knows why my parents sent me off every week day to integrate a wealthy suburban school or on a train ride with my maternal great-grandmother who barely tolerated or probably couldn't remember me because at brunch on Sundays and holidays with our large family one couldn't see much from the large dining room table to the third kids' table in the sun room?

By age I should have been at the second table just outside the dining room, but I was selected to oversee the littlest of the great grand kids. And even if I was old enough they would never let me sit at the kids' table in the corner of the dining room. I was demoted to the last table because they said that I interrupted the adults by asking too many questions and interjecting with trivial facts and comments.

So I was precocious. I was told that I was too smart for my own good. Actually I was the child who had to be bused, the little smart girl, literally and figuratively, who sat alone during recess and lunch because I was Black, and the little Black girl who was teased all the way home from school because she wasn't black enough. It's funny how skin color always seemed to figure in, like "Red," "Yellow," "Black," or terms like "Unfinished furniture." I was definitely relieved that it was summertime, and we were taking a family trip from Chicago to Washington, D. C.

Most summers once or twice a week, all eleven of us kids (five of mother's seven, four of her sister's, and two of her brother's), plus my Mom, would crowd into the gray Corvair and go visit my mother's grandparents in Hyde Park. What it meant for us was that we got to go over to the 57th St. Beach and the Museum of Science and Industry. I always seemed to get separated from the group. Something always caught my attention and I would turn, delay; or maybe, they were just too fast. Fortunately there was a fail safe for us, or me as it always turned out to be, that we would meet at the chicken incubator. The trick was how long it took them to realize I was really lost or just nearby.

Hyde Park was better than most fringe areas because of the University of Chicago which attracted liberals and tolerance, but there was always the chance of wandering into some area that you shouldn't be in Chicago. Several times we were chased home by rocks, bottles, or an onslaught of screaming people chasing after you because you were the wrong color or in the wrong ethnic area. One of the worst times was when we crossed into the Pullman roundhouse and nearby railroad, old factory, and wooded area about three blocks passed the imaginary race line just being curious. The area was about seven blocks from my cousins. Younger and older white kids started throwing rocks, bricks, and bottles at us. We started running and they chased after us with burning pieces of wood. Being last as usual I tripped and fell into a ditch about one block before safety. Everyone else was gone.

I lay in the dirt cringing under some over grown tree roots and weeds trying to suck back my breathing and tears as to not give myself away. Agonizing seconds turned into minutes as the opposition approached, "That'll teach them 'Nigs.' They won't be back here again." It took a long time for the voices to leave. I got cold and my ankle was sore and swollen. I tried to climb out but couldn't get a hold well enough and the ditch was too deep. About forty minutes later my family came back for me and pulled me out. I thanked them for crawling guerrilla style to rescue me. We did a three-legged hop all the way back, and got reprimanded on top of it. There were other times: the tennis courts at Marquette Park, the beach at South Shore, the picnic at Humboldt Park, the mall on Western, and the White Castles on Pulaski and Cicero only if you were in a group.

Although there was a lot of mobility into different areas in Chicago before and after World War II, most Blacks kept comfortably to the Westside, or the Southside like us. Talk during family meals from the older generation was, "Why go someplace where you weren't wanted; who needs any extra pain and aggravation? Need I say more?"

The younger side, from the table in the dining room, would counter, "What does that mean? What if it was a good opportunity, a nice place, and better schools?"

I chimed in from my perch around the corner, "It sounds like there is a story there?" Then immediately someone would start talking about what a nice meal this was; even though we had the same thing every Sunday.

We talked about many things during our large family brunches, but every time we got to the subject of busing, segregation, housing, the suburbs of Chicago, anything personal, some family incident, or an act of racism, a hush came over the group with eerie expressions of disdain for questioning teens. Shortly one of the young adults would ask for some food or condiment to be passed and the subject was changed.

Chicago had a past, a past of little tolerance. There were two significant race riots in Chicago, the 1919 Race Riot which started because a black teen crossed the imaginary line of 29th St. on the beach, and the 1951 Race Riot where Negroes tried to break the restrictive covenants and move into Cicero. This was the extent of my knowledge on the two incidents because even our immediate family talked about every subject over dinner save race.

The whites in the family really had no color to us until out in public. They were just our grandfathers, an aunt, or an uncle; there was nothing else said. Segregation; civil or voting rights, or lack of; the Black Panthers; the Nation of Islam; and Rev. Elijah Muhammad, who lived down the street in the house my father sold him, all were taboo. Even when I objected vehemently in tears, anger, and then protest (I refused to come out of my room for days until my supply of Pepsi and Jays potato chips ran out.) about being bused, my protestations fell on deaf ears. This would evoke about a fifty minute lecture on the value of education, wanting more, and not just wanting to be a victim of the times. Sure enough there was always one of those bad days where in tears I swore I would never go back to such a racist school, and then my mother would hug me, smile, and say, "Pick yourself up; dust yourself off, and start all over again."

The racial clashes in Chicago continued into the sixties over the use of schools, the beach, and parks. Now, the imaginary line was the beach area from 61st to 29th, the North side past Old Town, and anywhere west of Western, and the tension and fear of repercussion grew worse with each more western street you crossed from Kedzie to Pulaski. You were strictly warned not to venture into Mayor Daley's Bridgeport or to go past Cicero Avenue into Cicero. We even drove many miles out of the way to go to O'Hare Airport instead of Midway in Cicero.

Notwithstanding Chicago's own problems, the climate in the U. S. made for uneasy times for those of color. The 1954 legal victory in Brown vs. Board of Education; the murder of Emmitt Till in 1955; then the bus incident with Rosa Parks in 1956; Little Rock, Eisenhower's Civil Rights Act in 1957; sit-ins, marches, and sadly killings in Philadelphia, Mississippi, Birmingham, Washington, and Memphis. There came a slight period of hope until Medgar Evers' and President Kennedy's assassinations in 1963 then Malcolm X's in 1964. Even with King getting the Nobel Peace Prize and the Civil Rights Act of 1964 banning discrimination in employment practices and public accommodations, not much seemed to change. There was even talk about President Johnson passing the Voting Rights Act to force states to uphold the 15th Amendment. Sadly, it was still prevalent to see "Negroes Need Not Apply" when you went to a real estate office to buy a house or rent a place.

After the horrible spring with the Selma to Montgomery marchers being attacked by state troopers in March it looked like there wasn't going to be a peaceful summer. In my small world, the summer of 1965 started off well. Another semester of busing was over; no more uniforms, no more walking on eggshells. I could stay in my neighborhood, travel to different cities and see cultural exhibits and museums, read, and visit with my cousins.

It was the end of my aunt's medical residency and a belated wedding reception, so the entire family had driven to Washington, D. C. in several cars. My mother being a grade school teacher, and although pregnant, decided to take all of us kids as usual. We had a great time all the way to Washington.

It was a good time to spend with family. Normally our Sunday or holiday meals over our great-grandparents' house were wrought with such tension because we had to act as small adults not children. Only with my mother's sisters could we have fun and act our age at the zoo, museum, park, beach, and even in the house. The celebration was going well until a news flash mentioned a family being given the run around about a rental and a cross being burned on a new home owner's property.

My great-grandfather made a comment about his job never being done. My father squeezed his glass so hard that he broke it and cut his hand. He left the room and went into the dining room where my mother was, and she bandaged it up. My great-grandfather George followed, "What's your problem?" Dad went out the back door without comment. Mom went over to say to her grandfather, Papa, "Maybe you shouldn't say anything, like you've done all these years."

Papa said, "Even after all these years; I can't believe it."

Mom said, "You started it by fooling around with that white woman and almost getting everyone killed."

Papa quickly interjected; "Nothing happened; it was all in her head."

Mom replied, "I don't mean romantically; you just should have figured out that she was crazy early on. With Grandma's death, Mother being hurt, hiding the kids, and all of the threats, we barely made it through that year, all of us, but especially him. You got on with your life while we have struggled ever since." Mother Adams came in, and everyone went about their business quietly like nothing happened.

I had followed and asked, "What's wrong with Dad? Is he mad at Papa?"

Mother Adams looked at me.

Mom said, "It was about the Cicero Riot back in 1951. Your great-grandfather and father were victims of it, even though they were blamed for causing the riot and several other things."

Mother Adams changed the subject talking about where my mother was going to send the kids to stay while under "bed rest."

With a prior miscarriage which needed extensive surgery, and having difficulties during the trip, she, my father, and doctors thought it best if the kids were farmed off to relatives and she would fly back home while someone else would drive her car back. To give her an extra break during "bed rest," each of us was to spend the rest of the summer with a relative.

I must have missed the discussion or volunteering of who would go with whom because I surely would have stayed with one of my aunts. I don't know why I got this relative, my great-grandmother, Minerva Jewell (nee Lampton) Adams, at 76.

From Sunday and holiday brunches, I only knew a scowl, a closed eye, and a hand being raised. We couldn't eat before going to Catholic Church if you wanted to receive Communion, and arriving famished after sitting an hour and a half did not help. What a nice pleasant person she was when offering to take me because my mother was having twins, her seventh and eighth child!

I didn't think that I was an evil person or had done something so reprehensible at my age, but some punishment was being exacted. I would never ever contradict or interrupt with some tidbit of knowledge ever, ever again! As soon as I finished waving to my parents from the train window my sentence began.

"Enough, now. Ladies don't give 'P. D. A. s'."

"What is a 'P. D. A.'?"

"Public display of affection. Never show your emotions and don't let any mannerism give away who you truly are or as a leg up for someone to take advantage of, especially as you grow to become a lady, and you have a long way to go, literally and figuratively," as she shook her head.

"But, why? Isn't showing one's emotions towards someone you care about the whole point? Who cares who's looking? If someone has a problem with it, it's because they probably are jealous, lonely, or both. I would be happy, no blessed that someone kissed me on the cheek, gave me a hug, or waved and smiled sadly, or even cried goodbye."

"Right now you're too loud, and you're being snide. Children should be seen not heard. Sit down; read a book." I guess she was wondering why she got me, too.

"I don't want to read. I want to look at the scenery and walk through the train. Can we please look around? This is my first train ride."

Her eyes sternly looked at me, and without even a flinch said, "No."

"Please? Pretty please? I won't ask for anything else. Please?"

"No, I said no. What part of no don't you understand?"

"But,"

"I said No, N-o-e, no!"

I tucked my head and tail, plopping into my seat on the aisle. How mean and embarrassing! She said it loudly enough for everyone to hear, and she couldn't even spell such a simple word. It wasn't a big request. I'm stuck with her for hours, and she won't even let me sit by the window. Lord knows what I did to deserve being trapped for eighteen hours.

What was her problem? Why would she take me for three months when she seemingly didn't care for children? I don't ever remember any extemporaneous signs of affection or deed other than the brief hug when you came over for brunch. Everyone even seemed to be kicked out after a couple of hours. We would then have dinner at home or at another relative's. As a matter of fact, I don't ever remember anyone mentioning her coming out East until she showed up on the doorstep where we were staying in DC. And it was my bad luck to answer the door.

Talk about from bad to worse or no luck at all. Her first words were, "Well, you must be the one to stay with me. I said whichever little one opened the door was the one I wanted."

There she was like a shiny penny on the ground. Her roly-poly full figure draped in a silk dress with satin shoes to match made me think that she missed a ritzy funeral. The reddish ecru skin was like you have never seen in a perfectly blended tone. Her long jet black hair was rolled down in a bun, and she peered over gold rim glasses tethered by a small woven sash.

After squeezing me half to death in her immense bosoms, and kissing me full of the reddest rouge that I had ever seen, she made me carry her bags up to the third floor.

As soon as I made it back down the stairs exhausted and in pain, she tore into me, "It's a good thing you'll be with me this summer. I couldn't even tell you were a little girl." She whisked off my baseball cap, took out a brush and pulled my hair into the tightest ponytail. I ran to the mirror to see if she had pulled out any hair.

"There, at least your hair looks more ladylike. We'll have to do something with those jeans and tee shirt. Make sure they're not in your bag for the trip."

I hollered, "Mom, your grandmother is here."

Minerva froze just before she finished "lighting" into me. She turned a pale shade of green, and slumped towards the sofa. I tried to revive her, but she didn't come to.

"Mom, something's happened to your grandmother! Come quickly! She doesn't seem to be breathing."

Just as I got out the last few words she came back mid-sentence, "Hush, child! Have you lost your mind? Where's your home training? I know your mother got it, so what's your excuse? Either go and get her or wait for her to come. She knows I'm here."

"I'll take your suggestion, and I'll go get her. Besides, I've got to go practice my tennis game at the park. I'll see you at dinner." I quickly exited before she got one more negative word out of her mouth.

After changing and on my way out, I beseeched my mother, "Mom, do I really have to go with her? The last few minutes were like tying my loose tooth to a string and the doorknob. A weekend would be like playing a match with dead balls, better still, 'dog balls.' I can't imagine a whole summer. What about tennis, and my friends? I can really help you out with the twins. I can cook, and get things for you. How will you get around with Dad at work? Or, let me stay here in DC?"

"Your sister will be back from college next week and she'll be able to do all those things. It will be all right; just give it a chance. Your great-grandmother is a little strict. She looked after me and your aunts. See, we turned out fine," as two of her sisters smiled, and my mother touched my face. "Aren't you going out to practice, so you can make it back to go to the Smithsonian with the group? Go on; be back before lunch."

I changed into my shorts and t-shirt, grabbed my two wooden racquets in their presses and covers, and my laundry bag of balls. I turned the corner after jumping down the last two steps passing through the kitchen to go out the back door trying to avoid the wicked witch, and "Bammm!"

I ran smack dab into her. "See, child! This will have to stop. You're a shame to your family. Being a tomboy will never get you a husband."

"Mom!" My great-grandmother had my ear, and wouldn't let go. "Sorry, I was just late. I really have to go, please."

My mother turned from the stove to say, "Grams, she's okay. She's anxious over being late. She hates to be late, especially for tennis. She's a good girl. I'm really blessed to have her. She helps me out, as well as all of her brothers and sisters."

Quickly I made a beeline for the door. I ran all the way to Rock Creek Park without looking back the entire half mile. I hit the old, dingy balls I carried in my sack over and over again imagining her face on each shot.

As the sun peered through the trees at the edge of the court, a couple appeared and frowned with disapproval at my being on the clay courts even though I had on my whites. They commented, "The courts are for members only."

I said yes, "That's what my uncle said when he gave me his membership number to sign in with." Oh, I loved doing that! I'm sure it would get back, and I would be reprimanded. So, I gathered up my things and headed in, for the next day I'd be running circles in my mind, wrestling a gator in the bayou for the right to live while trying to get back home.

There isn't a family resemblance in any features between my great-grandmother and me, and the most obvious of skin tone blows my mind. Any outsider could never guess that we are related. My mother, her parents and siblings stayed with grandparents Minerva and George Adams at times, or lived in one of their properties at other times, such as 5138 South Kenwood, where I would stay. This one property was the four story home built by Paul Cornell founder and owner of Hyde Park before it became part of Chicago for his daughter Elizabeth in 1885 for pennies on the dollar. Of course my life and the value of my summer seemed to be less than a penny. I hoped that the motion of the train would soon put one of us to sleep, the only welcome relief to my misery.

"Clank! Clank!" Then came five seconds of the wind rushing by the car. "Clank! Clank!" The same cadence pounded over and over again.

I jumped up as the silence and obedience had grated their nails across the blackboard of my brain. Slowly I lifted up trying to inch my way past the wolf that had me cornered and pinned by her legs.

Just before jumping for freedom, I noticed a huge man asleep in the seat behind me. Already having sprung off the seat, I had to do a 360-degree spin to avoid him and land in the aisle. I landed slightly askew, twisting my ankle. As I hobbled to the door, bracing myself to open it and pass between the cars, the porter brushed by.

I hurriedly limped by in search of the observation car. On the way I passed through the club car, giving a glimpse of my destination.

It was worth the excruciating climb. By the time I got situated we were in the Allegheny Mountains of Pennsylvania.

It was such a beautiful panorama. I wish that I had seen more before the yawns, frustration, and sleep took over. "Helyn, Helyn Marguerite, wake up! Didn't you hear me say stay in your seat? I've been looking all over for you." Ouch, there was the proverbial middle name which meant I was in too deep, in trouble, and all was to hit the fan and me!

It seemed like she thought about something as she hesitated in my scolding, before yanking me up out of my seat by my ear. As I passed her, she swatted my behind with a rolled up newspaper; "For disobeying; wham!" She dragged me forward and hit my legs producing a red whelp. "I directly forbade you to come here."

"No, you just said that I couldn't sightsee when I asked earlier. This wasn't the same thing."

Then, "Whack!" She smacked the back of my neck with her open palm.

Tears rolled down. In between sniffles I whimpered, "What was that for?"

"Say another word and it will be worse, and if you don't stop crying now and causing a scene, then I'll give you something to cry about." She might as well go the full nine because from what I've experienced in the past several hours generated no familiarity or bonding, only contempt and irritability.

I opened my mouth and shut it as she wrinkled her eye and twitched her arm as to raise it. Sucking in my tears, I thought what a witch, and pouted. "And this little piggy went 'Wee, wee' all the way," back to my seat, and home.

No sooner then arriving at the four-story in Hyde Park, did I call home. Not to say that I had arrived safely, but that I needed to be rescued. "Please Mom, can I come home? It was terrible on the train. She wouldn't let me do anything. All I wanted to do was to go to the observation car, and she went off. This is impossible! Can you tell her to let me take the bus back home?"

The phone left my hand faster than the fried chicken left the bones on the ride to Chicago. "She's fine. We're fine. I'll call next week," as the old black dial phone hit the cradle. "Go unpack your things. I want you to go to the store for me."

"What store? I don't know where the store is."

"I'll take you. After that, you'll have to get there on your own as one of your chores. I like fresh food every day."

The large house was in Hyde Park, only a few blocks from the University of Chicago. We walked down one block to the corner store, and everywhere that I turned it seemed that we were the only ones. The small store that we entered seemed to have a little of everything. Minerva peered over her glasses at me, "There's an art to picking vegetables. You have to look at their color and shape, size them up by touch and smell. If you're lucky they'll have an exquisite taste, smooth texture, and encompassing aroma to excite your palette and tickle your fancy, much like people. That's why I said your appearance told me your whole story when I first saw you."

"Intelligence, culture, and beauty hidden by denim, lack of gender, and too much mouth and individualism. You're not a pleasant experience because of your roughness. You have to develop some style, even an iota will get you by."

"I have to defend myself from people who bother me in school and on the way to and from school, and I have to compete every weekend against older kids on the tennis court, moreover, on the court and in school, I vie for credibility as the only black. This is me; that's my world."

She stopped the conversation because I was getting worked up. However, once back at home, "What can you say or show for yourself that leads me to know that you're a bright, smart girl from a good family? Can you cook or sew? What boy or man do you think would be interested in you like this?"

She took me in front of the mirror on the hallway closet door. I had on a plaid camp shirt, red Keds, no socks, and rolled up jeans. "It's functional, and I'm not interested in any boys. All they do is bother me, and try to sneak a kiss."

"We'll change all of that. Let's make dinner before Mister comes home."

"You mean Papa or Great-Grandpa Adams?"

"'Papa' will be just fine."

I didn't see what all the reverence was meant to be, but we hurried to cook Sunday's meal of fried chicken with tons of seasoning in the pressure cooker, rolls, corn, green beans, and orange juice mixed with a thick grape wine. Also, it meant a reprieve by having other family members for support. Once the meal was ready we had to go and change, as Minerva said, "Belles always dress for meals, especially on Sundays."

She made me go in and take a bath, which I didn't mind so much, but when I came out in a towel, most of my clothes were gone. The only thing on the bed was a calico dress with an apron. Ugly didn't say enough. I marched to the kitchen dripping all the way, to find my great-grandmother putting my clothes down the laundry chute. "No," I shouted! Don't do that." My great-grandmother went about her business. I suppose being deaf and unemotional were advantages as the worker outside the padded cell, and pretending not to hear was a tool in getting her way.

After running back to my room, I cried for twenty minutes until she came in, and insisted that I get dressed. If I obeyed her she would find something appropriate for me to wear around the house or to play tennis in. She countered with, "But, only if you get dressed quickly and behave."

I conceded, broken, hungry, and stunned but mostly making the effort to see my cousins and other family members. Alas, most were still traveling or tired from the trip; it was just me. I flopped down in my seat at the dinner table, letting out a crude noise. An evil glance came my way, and I blurted out, "It wasn't me. It was the plastic!"

We sat at the table until Papa came in. He was this tall, imposing man with straight jet black hair, glasses, bow tie, and summer suit, as pale as he could be. He didn't say anything. Most often he didn't speak many pleasantries. But once discussions were open he would expound. He bowed his head and rubbed his hands together back and forth, over and over again for a minute, and then said, "Let's eat."

I stared very rudely trying to make out the two bookends that I was positioned in between. Dinner was short without words being said unlike home where there were three or four conversations going on at the same time. There was constant movement of some dish or condiment being passed, and what transpired in each one's day's activities. Here even the breathing was meant to be silent. Thirty minutes into the meal as I was about to bolt; he talked. A hand was put on my shoulder and I re-took my seat. "Today we will learn how to invest money and read the stock market."

I listened but I didn't really want to, so it didn't sink in. However, after the fourth time, I sort of got into it. Mom said that they had a maid, but usually on Sundays when we were there I didn't see anyone. It must have been her day off, and since most of the extended family was still in DC or traveling there was no reprieve. What it meant more than anything else is that I had to do the dishes and clean up all by myself. Once I was done, I was told to bring out the pound cake with raspberries and Neapolitan ice cream. This by far was the best part of my trying day.

Afterwards they just sat in the living room and read books. There they were propped up in two beautiful pink silk chairs accessorized in plastic. The drapes behind them were a lighter pink with gold thread interwoven with an outer plastic wrap. They read by the light of a red china lamp with gold inserts and gold threads in the shade accented by plastic. On the floor was a deep plush tan carpet with plastic runners hiding the bulk of it. I was puzzled that a childless couple had plastic on everything.

Obviously they could afford beautiful and costly furniture, but what was the point of having it if you couldn't enjoy it. Plastic, it's awful smell, offensive sounds, and irritating feel, was all I was experiencing. I wondered what silk or fine upholstery felt like.

I asked about watching the television, and I got the response, "It isn't for children." So, bedtime came earlier than I would have liked. It was a small black and white TV in a tan cabinet with a stereo record player in the foyer across from the main doorway.

My room was just off the foyer so I planned to sneak a peak at some point in the night. While falling off to sleep, I ported to the fall with the teacher asking, "What did you do for your summer vacation?" My response would be, "I cried from sunset to daybreak, and ached for the times when I could be the dog hanging out the car's window."

A large rotund woman woke me up the next morning at six o'clock for breakfast. With her German accent, she said, "I'm Erna. It's time to get dressed and come out for breakfast." Slumbering into the bathroom, I pulled my sweats over my nightshirt and went out to eat. I took the long way to the kitchen, going down the long hallway that led past another bedroom then back to the master suite through another hallway to the servant's quarters, then back to the kitchen.

During the day, Erna usually cleaned and waited on them, but now her responsibilities included looking after me. Erna's broken English and German were hard to understand, but her smile and welcoming gestures were evident through the storm that I was in. What's more, her stout figure and gray hair made her look like Mrs. Claus.

Heated plates were served and set on the table. While we were waiting, Erna peered from behind the butler's pantry. She had the swinging door ajar just ever so slightly.

Mister nodded, and Erna came scampering out with the food. He didn't speak but motioned for Erna to put me in a chair on the side. As soon as I sat down, Mister sat four clear boxes with something inside them down on the table. Seventeen minutes went by until Madam came out and sat opposite of George. Without pomp or circumstance he started to speak.

"I want to introduce you to some new vitamins. There's one for everything you need. They're by Viasin and all natural, sugar-free, and without preservatives. I just bought the company; you can oversee it, and I'm going to hire people to distribute them for you."

Madam replied, "Do you think anyone at the office or the detective agency will want some? If not, they can be sold on the weekend."

He replied, "Not sure, but I just put out $1,000, so we definitely will see. Just because I'm the owner of both and the senior partner doesn't mean that they will necessarily buy them from you. It's just how it is, but we'll keep that quiet."

Erna came in, "Sir, it's time."

He looked at his pocket watch, grabbed his briefcase, and put his fedora on his head. Madam sat still without another word, while Erna went scurrying off to take breakfast off the dining room table. They had a kitchen table, but no one ate there. On his way out he turned back, reached into his wallet and gave Mother Adams a $20 bill.

Erna took me with her on her daily chores as she walked around the streets of Hyde Park with its small shops and café style restaurants filled with university students and faculty. The bakery shop was our first stop, then we went on to the cobbler who sharpened knives for us on his wheel, then to the farmer's market for fruits and vegetables, and on the way back we stopped at the butchers.

The butcher was German, too, and he and Erna excitedly talked for several minutes. Before she could introduce me, another shopper came up and complimented her on her beautiful child. Erna said thank you in German, and continued talking. Then she introduced me to her friend, and we both said hello. He was very kind, and offered me a peppermint inside a dill pickle. It was strange, but tasty. After collecting our sauerkraut and other sausages, we went back to the house.

My great-grandmother had already left when we got back in. I helped Erna unpack and she made lunch. She put the sausage in the water to boil with the sauerkraut. Once it was done she put them on a hard Kaiser roll with lots of ketchup for me.

During lunch I asked, "Where did great-grandmother go?"

"Everyday Madam has her activities. Most days she takes the jitney to the elevated train on 51st then a bus and then a cab to the Arlington racetrack, and shops afterwards at Hillmans. At least once a week she goes to Mister's law offices downtown," Erna said.

"How long have you been with them?"

"For a time now, I think. I not so good with time and only a little better with the English."

"But, you're here. What city are you from in Germany? What about your family? I miss mine. Don't you miss yours? I want to go home, no offense. What's for dinner? When will great-grandmother get back?"

"Nein, nein. Okay." Erna had been so nice and talkative all day, then nothing.

"Whack!" My great-grandmother ambushed me, and hit my legs with a rolled up flyer that she had in her hand. It was nothing serious, but it definitely got my attention.

"What did I tell you about aggravating grown folks? Go in and get those shorts off. Put some pants on since it isn't Sunday. Erna did you take her around with you outside dressed like that?"

I interjected, "I'm not a kid. It's the sixties. I'm supposed to have shorts on in the summertime. Don't blow a gasket."

She wrestled my ear, and led me through the back door and down the stairs to a bush in the backyard. "Pick one and pull it out."

"Why? Why are you so mean to me? I didn't do anything wrong ask Erna."

"Pick a switch," as she tugged at my ear again. I did what she said. She swished the leaves off of the limb in a split second.

"Dance now. I'm going to make you dance," as she swatted my legs. I jumped repeatedly, rapidly, and with religion sniffing back tears and hatred. "See if you had put pants on, and obeyed me, then the switch wouldn't have hurt so badly."

Mine was a short dance, yet it felt like a pot of water that never seemed to boil. As soon as she released me, I ran up the stairs past Erna saying, "I hate her," just before slamming the door to my room.

I didn't come out the rest of the day. Around six o'clock, our scheduled dinnertime, just before George was scheduled to make his appearance, Erna came in to get me. "Child get dressed properly, then come out and eat. You got spanked. Learn from it and get on with it. They're not really mean, but they do mean for you to do as they say. Hurry, it's almost time."

Erna pulled out a shirt and some peddle pushers for me to put on as I brushed my hair. I put the outfit on quickly, and we both made it back seconds before he pulled out his watch to signal his greeting and prayer.

George shocked everyone when he said, "Madam, why don't you bring her down to the office, so she can meet everyone and possibly help out after she does her chores of taking care of the birds and plants in the front sun parlor. I have a case to go to the Supreme Court and she can help with the copying. My associates will be out tomorrow."

She said, "I remember one of your first cases that went to the Supreme Court back in 1922 that you won. I'll bring her down if you think that it is a good idea."

The next day we went downtown on the "El," or Loop elevated train to 30 W. Washington. I kept quiet, and she left me alone. When we got to the office, Minerva went over to the receptionist to see Attorney George C. Adams. She didn't ask to speak to him as a wife, but more as a client.

Sure enough, she was announced as a client to see him. When he stepped out he called her by her maiden name, Minerva Young. We went in and I had my mouth open as I toured the museum of photos and certificates.

I continued pouring over all the plaques and certificates hanging on his wall which were:
- Presidential Certificates of Appreciation:
    - Signed by Franklin D. Roosevelt & Lewis B. Hershey: One for 4 yrs., One for 2 yrs., One for 1 Yr.
    - Signed by Dwight D. Eisenhower Awarded in Washington, DC on March 31, 1957
- The Selective Service Medal - Congressional Certificate of Merit, Signed by Harry S. Truman & Lewis B. Hershey
- Presidential Appointment as Government Appeal Agent – 1965 by Lyndon B. Johnson, Local Board #4 – Chicago, IL
- Founder of the National Bar Association in 1925

- Publisher/Editor Chicago World and The Enterprise
- Bar of the Supreme Court, 1922 – Cornelius J. Jones
- Adams Secret Service Agency / Adams Detective Agency/Burns & Lloyd.

He never mentioned anything about helping out today, so we left by the same cloak that we came in with. We went out without a goodbye and went down the elevator to a nice store called Hillman's.

Minerva paused as she was opening the door, almost as if she was paralyzed. "Great-Grandma!" She fell into the door, breaking her fall.

A bagger was just inside and helped me get her to a nearby bench. He asked if I wanted him to call an ambulance. I said, "Let's give her a few minutes. I know she'll be fine. She's just got to."

Chapter Two
"Do As I Say"

I took a handkerchief out of her pocketbook, and wet it at the fountain inside the store. Almost ten minutes had gone by. I turned to call for help when I felt something grab my arm. I turned back, and her eyes were open, and out of one was a small tear.

She smoothed her face and lightened her mood so that a half smile was displayed. "You did fine child. I'm hungry. Let's get our food, then some popcorn at Garretts. You like popcorn don't you? It's caramel, butter, and cheese, real cheddar." Finally something positive, a reward!

We ate the triple popcorn, sharing one bag. On the bus ride home I got sleepy, and Minerva let me lean up against her all the way home. She told me about her friend Casey Jones, who grew up near her in Tennessee, and how he needed help one day with a horse. Her father helped him out and they played until it was time to go. She mentioned that she saw him several times on the Illinois Central Railroad. She never got to the end of the story because we arrived at home, and Erna ushered her to the back. At dinner that night she didn't say a word.

"Well, I want to tell you about my new talk show on radio station, WEAW. It's a news, commentary, and weather show. Why don't you come down and speak?"

Minerva never replied as she got up before dessert to go to her room.

I said, "She was a little sick on the way back from your office. I guess she's still a little tired."

George left, and Erna told me to go on to bed, and she would put everything up.

Things went smoothly for a period of one week, fourteen hours. I had practiced very little tennis except off the side of the garage with an old, not quite "dead" but close, tennis ball, when only Erna was home. Usually with the days starting so early by the time evening came I didn't mind that I missed TV.

Today for some reason I had some extra energy, so I planned to make my way to the foyer to watch the black and white television set, and hopefully catch the "Man from U.N.C.L.E.," since I missed the "Ed Sullivan Show" on Sunday. Now, I could actually relate to Topo Gigio; both our strings were being pulled as we gyrated all "topsy turvy" I cracked the door ever so slowly, while it moaned just like I would if I got caught. Fortunately my great-grandparents were so far in the back in their suite that even if I slammed the door I might not be heard.

I slithered across the floor as if it were a war torn beach. Finally turning on the set, waiting for the tubes to warm up, I basked in my accomplishment. I got even so cocky in my thoughts that I planned a raid on the ice box in the hallway outside the maid's quarters.

The fun wasn't so much about watching the tube, but in that I had control over one thing that I could do, and I finally got away with something. Not being an adult, everyone tells you what to do, and never asks if you like to do something. You learn how you fit in, while developing some interests and likes and dislikes attempting to master yourself and something, anything, in a confusing life and world.

While I was patting myself on the back, I saw a light inch its way into the corner of my eye. I turned off the TV set, and closed the doors. Their large bedroom door announced its function. Fear of being found out or punished froze me in my tracks.

I thought for sure that I was going to be busted. Yet, with the door halfway open, and the sweat from my body causing a puddle on the floor, there was nothing. I rose up to turn around, and hit my head on the cabinet door that had swung back open.

The pain rang my head causing me to abandon hope of getting away. Still no one. I closed the cabinet door, and I lifted to turn. There was a squeak. I paused, and still no one.

Every second I had my eyes trained on their door. When it moved again, I had just made it to my feet. I tiptoed back to my room, easing the door open and closed at the same time that they completely opened theirs. I scuttled into bed, pulling the covers over my head.

I relaxed thinking that I had made a clean getaway. There it was that long narrow dagger into me of light. My heart started beating like a drum in a march song. There was no way that I could get back across the rickety wooden floor that creaked even at the thought of you putting your foot down.

"Footsteps!" Then, they appeared. I held my breath trying not to be detected. The draft from the door chilled me, and the urge to sneeze pressed heavily upon me. I pinched my nose with one hand and covered it with the other.

The urge subsided as I caught a glimpse through the crack in the door. I could just barely see George and Minerva, who were all dressed up. The fear of my ordeal paled to the view of my great-grandmother in stark white make-up and white full-length satin gown escorted by my great-grandfather in a charcoal gray suit.

They hesitated next to my door. I thought that she saw my door ajar, because she turned her head ever so quickly toward it. My body started to shake, and a nervous twitch grappled my head and thoughts. Then the urge to go to the bathroom took over. I squeezed my legs, tucked in my body, and centered my thoughts. I thought of many other things, too many things.

The shivers increased so much that I wet my bed. I tried to hold it but the motion just wouldn't let go. This would be another case of disobedience. What punishment would this exact? God, I don't want to find out. More time went by.

She looked like she was trying to think of something to do to me. George stood between the door and a bad nightmare to say, "Come on, now. We cannot be late. There are three minutes to go and it takes two minutes to get downstairs. Are you ready?"

I chanted over and over again to myself, "Go. Go with him, please. Just, go!" Seconds turned into an awkward, smelly, and damp lifetime. Finally the door closed behind them, opening the floodgate of tears.

I got up out of my pool of disgrace and fear. Quickly I changed clothes and put them and the linen in the washer. Erna never came out, and God was good because I got everything dried and back the way it was just as the door opened again announcing their return. This time relief and exhaustion closed my eyes, without the pretense.

The next day we went through the morning ritual of breakfast: toast dipped in coffee, boiled Jones sausage links, and two minute eggs. Minerva must have sensed it was me spying on her and sneaking out of my room at night because she ignored me all day. I thought after our scary experience together that she would be more amiable and might include me in some of her daily jaunts. Not!

So, I went out on errands with Erna. "I understand that you were not so nice last night, and got into business that wasn't yours."

"I tried to watch the television set in the foyer."

"It wasn't yours, and you were told not to."

"I never have any fun. I just wanted to see one of the programs that I used to watch with my family. I wasn't trying to hurt anyone."

"Yes, but you disobeyed. Your great-grandmother takes things like that very seriously, as do I."

"You're not so uptight about it, though."

"Everyone is different based on their upbringing and experiences. Your great-grandmother was born to slaves who got their freedom only from Mr. Lincoln. Mr. Frank fought for a country that did not want him as a half-breed, and suffered much because of it in the 1800's. Your great-grandfather on the other hand talks very little about his childhood, but my understanding is that he is related to one of the President's. His mother had no last name on his birth certificate and he was left to someone in Virginia. They moved to Louisiana where he had to work for them as a servant at the same age as you are now."

"No, I didn't know any of that. No one talks about the past in our family. What about you?"

"My family was taken to a Nazi camp for Germans because we were helping Jews. That's where my parents and older brother died. I got out after seven years when the war was over. I was taken in by the church, and a few years ago I moved here to the States. I had no work and I met your great-grandmother on a bus stop in Chicago. We talked politely, and stood next to each other on our way to the Southside. Halfway into our ride she had a spell. She didn't talk or move for minutes. I helped her into a seat in the back of the bus. When she came to, she embraced me, and we have been friends ever since. She offered me a job, and I moved in with them. Here I am."

"When I go out with my great-grandmother everyone seems to stare. Some have made comments, or they move away, or they ask if I'm all right. Don't you feel strange when out with them or working for them? Doesn't it seem to be a lot of prejudice?"

"It's bad; it's true. There are people like that. The people, the Germans arrested us for helping, were neighbors that my family had lived next to for thirty some years. We celebrated with them birthdays, holidays, and sadly even some deaths. Yes, they were Jews, but we knew them as friends. You're great-grandparents have been fair to me, and we are friends."

"She's not fair to me."

"Child, child, have you tried to be fair to her, or understand, and not be so rebellious?"

"Speaking of the devil?"

"Don't ever say that!" Erna took me to the sink and washed my mouth out with soap. I lost my only ally. I went to my room in tears again.

Then a knock and Erna's voice, "It's time for dinner."

"I'm not hungry."

"That's not an option. Your feelings are hurt. Get on with it. You did something wrong, and you were punished. It doesn't change how I feel. Come now little one." Erna smiled with open arms. I washed my face, brushed my hair, and went to dinner.

Great-grandfather patted me on the head. I don't why, yet he did just before he told us about his new investment, a funeral home. "Everyone dies and pays taxes. What do you think Mother? Good idea?"

Minerva smiled, "Great idea. That's just what we will talk about on the radio station tonight."

"Just that," he said. "Life, death, and doing what's necessary to live in a society where you're not welcome, and barely tolerated."

I interjected, "What about the Civil Right's Movement, the Black Panthers, Angela Davis, King, or the Kennedys?"

"Hush girl. This is grown folks talk," he said.

"But, I experience the prejudice just like you. I see them looking at us, looking at you."

"You do? Look at you. You only have problems when you're with me," interjected Minerva.

"No. At home, some blacks make fun of me because of my hair, skin, and features. Or they tease me because of our large family and going to a Catholic school where I wear a uniform or at home where I wear hand me downs. When I get to school, with the whites, they make fun of me for the same thing, and raising my hand and having the highest grade point average. The only time I feel like I have a chance is on the tennis court."

"Enough, it's time to go. There are enough to champion that cause. We speak to those who get up, go to work, try to raise their families as God-fearing, and want better for themselves and their family. There'll be plenty of time for you to crusade. Enjoy being a child, and be fortunate that you don't have to work, be abused, or have to fight for life and freedom like we did. You're what this is all about." Without fanfare he offered his hand to Minerva. He looked at Erna, "Good dinner," and they left.

Erna put up the food, and I did the dishes. She went back to her room, and I fell asleep while reading some magazines at the table. One in particular, *Sepia Magazine*, had Mother Adams on the cover with an article, "The Woman Who Talked to the Dead." (Acheson, 1959) The article cited the famous people like Marilyn Monroe, Errol Flynn, Gen. George Marshall that she had talked to in her séances and readings. Also adding to the Sam Young legend is the fact that Al Capone and policy kings Iley Kelley and Ted Rowe sought her advice before and after their deaths. Skeptics brought translators who verified her speaking in nine authentic languages. At some point later Erna woke me up and got me to bed.

We started off early as usual, although not as early as during the school year where I got up at 4:30 AM to catch a bus then another bus and one last one. Another day into my month, and things had calmed down; no more dancing, but still no hugs.

Sunday came, and I requested to go to the Catholic Church down the street. Erna said that she would walk me there on her way to the bus stop and her church. On the way out, Great-grandmother said, "Now you look like a lady. That's a better outer and inner you," as I walked out in my dress, white laced socks, and patent leather shoes.

She gave me a dime for the offering. I was definitely trying to earn some "brownie points," because the dress and Shirley Temple curls were so hard to take.

My reprieve came at one with visitors, but no pardon. That evening my great-grandparents went off to their church or meeting, or something, downstairs. I wanted so badly to go, but decided against it in order to save myself any undue stress and hardships, let's be honest, whelps. I sat watching the blank television console until time to go to bed.

On Friday, with no incidents to my name, after she got $20 from Papa at the breakfast table, Great-grandmother suggested that I help her out for the day. I put my jeans on and a collared shirt with some loafers. We caught a bus to the elevated train to the Loop, and then switched to another "El" out to the Arlington Race Track. Once in, we got the "Red" and "Green Sheets" which she used to teach me how to handicap a horse. I picked six straight with four winners.

She picked up the winnings, more than tripling her initial stake of twenty dollars; bought me lunch; and gave me a dime for my lucky picks. "I'll put another dime in your coin saver portfolio for you. Remember the talk the other day by Mister about saving and leveraging your money. Most importantly, even though your great-grandfather makes good money, a girl's got to have her own." She laughed, and I smiled back as I ate my hot dog.

Feeling confident I asked, "Why don't you go to Hawthorne Racetrack in Cicero; it's closer?" She never acknowledged the question, so I continued eating.

I was so busy enjoying my hot dog with everything on it, that I didn't notice that Great-grandmother was having another spell. This time she was frozen with her eyes open, but was breathing steadily, so I waited a little while longer before getting help. When the gun went off for the next race, she closed her eyes, but I still couldn't wake her.

I went to phone my great-grandfather at his office. He said that he would be there quickly, and for me to stay with her and not to call an ambulance. An hour and ten minutes later, he approached with smelling salts. As he waved the salts under her nose, I told him, "The last couple of times she came to within a few minutes, and the next time a little longer. The spells seem to be getting longer. What's wrong with her? Have the doctors said anything?"

"We haven't quite figured it out yet, and the doctors say nothing is medically wrong with her. She's been like this for the past year, with the spells maybe once a month. Now they are about once a week, so we started hypnosis in the church. We'll figure it out."

He started to turn her sideways so that they could face each other. Then I saw a snub nose .38 revolver in a side holster. He asked me to help, but I froze staring at his gun.

He looked at me, and followed my eyes. "I'm a private detective, too, with my own agency. Mostly though I carry the gun because of work and the threats I get from former cases and clients."

"Why does a lawyer need a gun?"

"It's the times. If I go to the white neighborhoods to interview clients, every now and then, someone thinks I'm black. In the black neighborhood, someone will think that I'm white. There is always someone who just won't let you or some things be. Your father and I had a hard time with one case before you were born where we almost died and lost just about everything else. They even accused and indicted us for starting a riot by renting property to a black family in Cicero. We took a beating in the courts, our pockets, the press, and public opinion. A profitable business was dissolved. Since then there have been other incidents, and someone even tried to steal my Packard."

"Tell me what happened please? I am really interested. Dad never mentions the incident; only that thing in DC. I did notice your detective license for the Adams Detective Agency and your L. L. B. from Howard Law as well as certificates and pictures on the walls in your office. I saw some signed pictures with Dirksen, Stevenson, and McArthur."

"I'm a special officer in Oklahoma and a board member of the Selective Service System. I got a Congressional Medal and Certificate from Harry S. Truman, as well as other awards."

"Wow, I didn't know. Mom and Dad never said anything."

"Your father's still mad over a business deal. It was a good investment, but things on paper sometimes aren't what they turn out to be in our perfunctory world. Maybe one day he'll tell you the story. It's better that it comes from him. Come on now; times a wasting. We have to help Mother."

We turned her around, and he sat directly in front of her at the concessions. He touched her face on both sides with open hands. After taking his glasses off and putting them in his pocket, he spoke, "You're in a deep sleep. When I snap my fingers you will awake completely rested, remembering everything."

She opened her eyes upon hearing his voice. He continued, "When I count to three and snap my fingers, you will come out of your trance. One, two, three," and he snapped his fingers.

She awoke, and they embraced immediately. Trembling, she spoke, "I remember only seeing a woman's face this time. It was different than last time when the pain was excruciating. It was such a sharp pain in my foot, and then I just went numb, then frightfully cold."

"We'll see if we can make more progress this Sunday. What about doing something Wednesday evening? I'll see if we can reach everyone. Let's go home," he said.

"Sorry you had to leave the office," as Minerva collected herself.

"I'm glad Helyn caught me. I had just arrived from court and I came back only to pick up some papers needed for a deposition tomorrow. This is more important. Come on child; let's get her out of here."

My great-grandparents each put an open hand on a cheek, smiled, and continued on. We lifted Minerva up, and George extended his arm. I gathered her purse, tickets, and scratch sheets.

Sunday after brunch, they invited me down to attend their services. "This time we're going to try something different than hypnosis. I think we have no other choice."

"Like what," as my eyes lit up?

"You can come only if you keep quiet, no moving around, no questions. Just be a bump on a log," he replied.

After I returned from Mass and donating my worldly wealth, I put a skirt and blouse on with my loafers. As they made their way down the long hallway, I started getting nervous. Minerva had on a long white dress with no veil. She had her face made up with a white powdery foundation with brown lipstick, and her hair was extra black. George had on a black suit, white shirt, and black bow tie, complimenting his wingtips.

Just before he opened the big front door to leave, he said, "I'm sure this is different than your Catholic Church. Only speak when directly addressed and asked to. If you see or hear anything out of the ordinary, do not make a noise, or be too shocked. If the church is full, you can sit at the piano with Mr. Smith."

Now I was trembling. Maybe this wasn't such a good idea after all. Maybe watching a blank TV screen had its advantages.

It was crowded, so I sat down with Mr. Smith on the few inches I scrounged up to put one cheek on whilst holding on to the edge of the stool with one hand and one foot extended for balance. That was a remarkable feat in itself because he was so huge that he took up the entire bench except eight inches. He was quite a jovial man. After being introduced he picked me up for a hug, and I bounced off his belly as a large spoon of gelatin hitting the bowl.

When he started playing the introductory music the piano shimmied and the vibration from the stool and his body motion made me pop up. Each time I had to regain my composure, footing, and decorum and subsequently fight back for my few inches. Thankfully the service started saving me from further embarrassment from the perspiration and sweat rolling down my face and soaking my shirt.

It was time for the Interlude to start when Mr. Smith started playing again. I could feel the piano and bench start to vibrate more and more as he picked up the inflection with each new chord. Then we started jumping up in a rhythmical affirmation of each note played. My bumper car of a ride started again with bolts, turns, and slides. I spent so much energy trying not to fall and keep the front of my skirt down that I was soaking wet at the end of the piece.

Just as the storm had passed with safe harbor in sight, I let go of the stool and relaxed. Seconds later while trying to find the same page as everyone else in the hymnal, I flew off the bench. My skirt flew up, mercifully showing only the slip that I almost didn't put on. The entire congregation turned and stared at me. I turned redder than the reddest tomato, or my great-grandmother's rouge.

Mr. Smith trying to hold back a laugh just couldn't. His belly gave him away as he said, "You might want to hold on. Better yet, just go with it, and bounce. You'll keep your balance, and give less exposure. I do get into my music and praising the Lord." He chuckled, gave me his hand, and kept punching the ivories with the other hand.

The crowd snickered, my great-grandfather clapped and rubbed his hands together loudly looking over his rims at me with great ire, and Rev. J. P. Campbell shook his head. Mr. Smith let the vibrato swell as he pounded the poor little keys again.

George called the meeting, and Minerva was introduced as Reverend Minerva Adams. They read some scriptures, sang a few songs, as I bounced my way closer to God. I had finally gotten my balance and sense of rhythm, and was enjoying a departure from the Latin verses I chanted earlier, when Mr. Smith got the spirit. He started singing and becoming even more animated. "Slop," this big glob of saliva landed on my face during a "Hallelujah, thank you Jesus."

"Aaagh!" I tried to keep it in, but the utter grossness of it wiped me out. He was so off into his thing that he no idea of the fallout. Again, I was center stage. I knew that I would be dancing a jig tonight or tomorrow.

After an hour and a half, without further humiliation, the services ended. Some of the members left. More candles were lit, and the lights were turned out. Rev. Adams went to sit in a large chair on the dais, and George went to the podium. "God we ask you to send us one of your dearly departed to act as our guide to the spiritual world. Please send us someone to lead us. We have so much to find out and we are not sure of our way. We want to find the spirit possessing Sister Adams."

"'Possessing,'" rescued me from my onslaught of germs and grossness, which I thought should have scared any demons away. There was a pause in the petitioning, then nothing.

George repeated his earlier words verbatim in a louder tone, and still nothing. After the third plea, the candles flickered. There was a chill and all the candles save one went out with a rush of wind. It then went completely dark for a minute, and without anyone's movement or assistance, all of the candles were re-lit. Gasps went out over the smaller group, and a "What the," from me.

There was nothing, and minutes later George pleaded for help again. Then there was just the one candle, a table waffling between baited breadths. Then a voice, "My name is Snowball. I have been sent to be your guide."

"What is your real name? Who are you," asked George?

"Yours is to journey and witness," professed Snowball.

The Reverend bent her head forward and then it rolled. With her eyes closed, she spoke in the same male childish voice as Snowball. "I will tell you a story."

Chapter Three
"Back In A Day"

    The kerosene lamp seemed so strange without the crystal vase sitting on top. Only the wick stood straight to the flickering flame as it danced across the room, liken an athlete about to close out her first huge win. This certainly wasn't the blue flame the mother reverend predicted that would come when two slaves well beyond childbearing years would give birth. Such an amber glow dimly lit the bed where the mother and midwife struggled to bring forth life in 1858.
    The shanty was no bigger than 7' by 11' with only a bed on a pallet, now raised by cinder blocks to help with the delivery. Normally, the blocks held the lamp, pitcher, and bowl for washing because tables weren't allowed. Today the bowl was used to catch the baby, and the pitcher to bring the hot water off the fire outside. Nails held up night clothes, and a makeshift desk held the Bible that was opened to record this next generation. The wood and clay of the home smelled "mildewy," just plain damp and moldy because the rain was upon the country and the house.
    It was February, with its winter rains, that came and just stayed, on and on, and on in Kentucky. Yet, the din of the rain hitting the roof was drowned out by the screaming and excruciating utterances from the mother to be, "Aaagh! Please good Jesus. Please Lordy! Aaaaagh!" It sounded only shriller and more foreboding than a slave being whipped. While in unison, belted orders came out, "Push! Push, damn it!" Every so many series, the midwife would say, "You've got to get the baby out, now; it's caught. It's turn'in blue! Now, push!" It would start over, and over again, like cadence, seven times over.
    Yes, twenty-six was not an age to have a baby, and Frank was thirty-three, especially in slave years, because you aged faster. Most saw the gray tip in around twenty from the toil, labor, sweat, stress, and

pain, and maybe a few years later, if you were in the big house. At thirty you were bent over, grayed, maimed, and most never saw forty. Life was just too tough. You died seeking freedom, of a broken spirit and heart, or simply without fanfare or grandeur, the most demeaning and crushing of all, though, was you lost the will to live.

One aged according to the events that took place in one's life. The scuffed knee, the whelp marks, the keloids on body parts, the nub for one finger, the sleepless nights, agonizing nightmares, and tortured soul were the badges of honor, strife, resilience, and if there truly was a God. What wanton place for hope; the hope of freedom, if not this life then in death, or maybe the next life, if you had any faith left.

The rocking chair told the same story of life, love, challenge, and struggle of the generations now and before, and yes, tonight, finally the future. The scratches on the arm were from the mother sitting in the chair praying for the father to live after his beating for supposedly looking at a white woman. All thanked Jesus that they hadn't seen him kiss her, because that "white woman," that "poor white trash" was his niece. The nicks on the sides were the plantation kids' heights as they grew. Mother, Lucendy, claimed them as a surrogate, whispering daily words that would help them stand one more day. The singed hole in the back was from the fire that burned the boat that brought the chair to America from France.

The deep crushed purple fabric outlined in gold surrey capped off the rich, deep mahogany wood that had such ornate figures carved into it. At the end of the arms were two dragons with fangs and tongues showing. They served as symbols of divine intervention which protected the weary who most times were thankful for God's salvation and mercy that allowed them to make it to a safe harbor, and let her be able to sit, just sit without notice or fanfare, to just be still or sometimes rock, to just sit in this chair – your chair, and be peaceful.

A birth, though, gave cause to celebrate despite this being one of the worst winters seen. The storms came early this year with heavy rains, flooding, and destruction of the harvest. Legend had it that if the rains came before spring as they did that it was a bad omen. Everything down in these circles had significance.

You hid the hairs that fell out or were in your comb, and buried any nail clippings, because they could be used by anyone for voodoo. Times were hard enough but if you irritated or annoyed anyone in the slightest, a curse would be put upon you. If you were truly obnoxious then they would cast a spell upon your entire family. Pray to God that no one damned you and all of your ancestors.

In reverse they did the same for good luck, paper in sugar water, a string tied around a wrist, a chicken bone split. You jumped over a puddle, and never split a tree, and threw salt over your shoulder for any mishap. Luck, if not prayers, were needed to make it as a slave, and a new born child without freedom.

The baby came after a long and arduous labor of thirty hours. After the baby was wrapped and wiped, the mother passed out. The mid-wife tried to revive her, but to no avail. Suddenly the mother's body twisted and wiggled. Then out came a thunderous roar of a scream that sounded like a crime of murder followed by, "Sweet, Lordy Jesus, please! Oh my God!"

Minutes later the woman crowned again, and to everyone's surprise a foot appeared. In shock the mid-wife almost dropped the first child as she was cutting the cord. She exclaimed, "It's another one, but Lord help her; it's a breach. This one is ready to go feet first. Don't push! I don't think she would survive my cutting her, so I'll have to reach up there and turn the baby around."

She handed the first born to the father, Frank, and asked that prayers be said because the other baby already looked dead, and oh so pale. She poured the remaining hot water over her hands and then reached elbow high up pushing the baby back in and turning it around.

The father shouted, "Hurry. She's getting worse and the baby will die." Time ticked by like the ember escaping the fire. The mother bled profusely and started to moan in pain.

Finally, she said, "I've got it! Push now! We've got to get this one out quickly." Nothing. So, she took the baby's head and pulled it. She went flying back across the room into the door.

"Are you okay," asked the father?

"Yes, but she's gotta push," said the mid-wife. He pressed against the womb as she grabbed the head. Out popped the baby. A hush fell over everyone when they saw the color of the baby. It was as white as the clouds in the sky.

Surely it wasn't Frank's. Frank was close to the corn shucks during winter, but not Lucendy who was a brownish red from her Creek ancestors. There was only one explanation, and he sunk into the chair. Surely not his beloved Lucinda would lay with the master. He loved her and he knew she loved him, but why would she betray him.

Sure she was amiable and occasionally agreeable to appease them, the Johnsons. No, she would never lay down with them, especially him, even with the threat of impending death.

Master Johnson was bent over, skinny, pale as could be, more white hair on his face and body than his head. He reeked of the corn liquor that he would let the slaves have to keep peace, not the good brown stuff sold for profit.

How could Frank, who was looked upon by most as the leader, face "them folks" with one of the half breeds, the "Spots" as Master Johnson called them? He had laid with every woman and girl in childbearing years to aide in his socialization of the colored's, or in his words, "gentrification."

He plopped down with the weight of the world into that old rocker almost breaking it. You could see the tears well up in his eyes as he clung to his newborn daughter. He groaned, "She would die first before doing this to me. After what he did to her sister and mother, she swore to kill him if he laid a hand on her. Now, I will do it for her." He rocked determinedly at a frantic pace.

The mid-wife continued to clean the baby, hoping the mother had just passed out. She offered the baby to Frank, and he refused to take the baby. He asked, "Is she up, yet? I ache for an answer. I've just got to speak to her to find out how this came to be, and why she never told me, before I get my machete."

The mid-wife got some smelling salts trying to revive Lucendy, but nothing. Then she got some cold damp rags from out of the rain and put them on her forehead. Still there was no response.

He went to the pallet and screamed, "Mother talk to me. Don't leave me like this! Lord, she was the only thing that kept me sane and wanting to live."

Someone had gone to get the priestess earlier. She now put candles all around the bed, hung feathers over the mother's head, and placed mud on her forehead. Nothing.

The wind blew the shanty door open spraying the heavy rains upon everyone. The mid-wife covered up the pale child by pulling up her skirt. Frank turned his back to the storm to protect the baby and hide his tears. His Lucinda was gone. They had survived, all of these years of torture in Kentucky captive to two mad owners.

Frank spoke, "He's a dead man, as he grabbed his machete." To make matters worse, Johnson had given him his word to set him free at thirteen, but reneged. Every year for twenty years he asked and pleaded; not even a word. Mr. Johnson depended on Frank too much. All of these thoughts raged through his head.

The mid-wife said, "No, you have two healthy little girls to take care of," as she pushed the pale child to his chest with the brown one.

"Get that thing from me. I only have one, and I'll name her Mary." He handed Mary over to the priestess, "Here you take care of her. I won't be back. After I kill him, I'll have to go hide out in the mountains until I can make it up North, or they catch and kill me. One day, I'll be back for her." He stormed out into the pouring rain as a clap of thunder lit his way to the big house.

The mid-wife told one of the boys to run to the other side of the plantation to get word to the children of their sisters, since the sisters had killed themselves from shame after child-birth. If they could reach them, maybe one could take the pale one, whom she named Mollie, as the last sparkle went out her mother's eyes. The boy took the baby wrapped in Albertine's petticoat to the other compound.

Word spread throughout the colored area. No one came out save one friend who tried to stop Frank. He ran in front pleading with him not to do this, that they needed a leader, a live one. Frank pushed him to the side, and he slipped in the mud and hit his head, but he rose and continued walking. He had already reached the plank.

He reached the big house, and by then the dogs were barking, causing a commotion. Frank kicked down the door, and climbed the stairs where he found Silas Johnson in bed alone for once. He raised his machete to kill him, and an overseer stabbed him in his back.

Frank turned on him and killed him in one fell swoop by lopping off his head. He turned reeling in distress towards Silas. As he raised his arms to puncture his chest he fell from the wound and loss of blood directly on Master Johnson's johnson, severing it. There was some justice in a cruel world to save so many other girls from being raped.

As he was passing out, Frank recalled that just yesterday, Master Johnson shouted at his roly-poly wife that, "I'm doing the Lord's work. What's it to you? You do the Lord's work your way, and I'll do it my way. Besides, if all of them were mixed with white blood they'd be humanized and civilized. That's what I'm doing. The angel came to me and told me to lay with each and every one of the heathens so that I would get more riches and 'come uppance' on my judgment day. That's just what I'm do'in."

Mrs. Johnson's jet black hair was the only thing that looked young, because the wrinkles were prune like and her teeth brown from age and the corn pipe that she would smoke as she cursed and rocked on the porch at her "Darkies," as she called them. Every Wednesday evening, Sunday morning, daily at noon, she would go to services and, or meetings there to talk about suppressing the North, punishing runaway slaves, and keeping her property that her daddy left her, and his grand-daddy left him. Secretly her mission meant keeping Silas in his place and keeping his bastards from having an identity.

No one, or their secrets, tiptoed softly amongst the slaves. What made matters worse was that the plantation itself was in a state of upheaval even before Frank sought justice. Frank was a farmer; it was he who farmed the grain for liquor. Sadly, production was down because the rains came early causing the grains to rot. Instead of blaming this on the weather and bad luck, Johnson blamed Frank and the workers.

Whether they were at fault righteously or not, someone got whipped, or died. If you questioned an order or anything was out of place you were whipped; if you stole anything or moved your hand even slightly in aggression or defense it was cut off.

The Johnsons, lords of the manor and plantation, represented the elite of American born good southern gentry, not those foreign, righteous ones who showed some tolerance for the "colored," especially the "Mullatos." Their marriage was arranged for them at 14 for her and 31 for him. They never even consummated their marriage even on their wedding night. She was too afraid, and he too drunk to care. Times afterward they pushed their causes of gentrification and cleansing. Mostly, it was their contempt of each other, especially after he touched one of those, "Dark witches from Satan trying to ruin her."

Their bizarre and mostly warped notions of being European civilization's saviors rubber stamped their sins of vanity, avarice, and lust. Moreover, their condescending nature of being higher up on the food chain was downright nauseating.

Mr. Johnson's white workers dragged poor Frank by his feet down the hall to the stairway with blood trailing down the mahogany floor. As the supervisor got to the railing, Mrs. Johnson came trotting out, "See who's got the better plan. Your oldest and best darkie just tried to kill you. You, going around lying with all those dogs. Yeah, you've got fleas and they're big ones."

"Woman, get me a doctor! Send one of the boys to fetch him before I bleed to death. Remember your old daddy drunk all your peoples' money that's why they picked me. Remember? Now, get me some sheets and corn whiskey and sour mash."

She retorted, "Why, you only drink that clear stuff, that moonshine?"

"I need one to numb me, and the other to numb it." Mrs. Johnson called one of the house servants to get the liquor. The irony of it all was that it was Frank's niece who brought the bottles back, unbeknownst her.

Frank was shackled and dragged out to the stables. The supervisor and the only two other whites on the property mulled over what to do next. "Let's string him up by his feet until we find out what Mr. Johnson wants us to do. No one will bother him or do anything in this pouring rain," said the supervisor. The men did just that and went back to the main house.

The doctor came and treated Mr. Johnson, asking one of his white bosses, "Go retrieve his part. I'll sew it on with needle and thread. Maybe it will take." The man came back empty handed.

The bleeding had taken a toll, but Mr. Johnson put under with his favorite rot gut slinked off into grogginess. Before passing out he told the three to round up all the Mandingoes so that they could see Frank strung up. The colored were forced out into the rain as they were rousted out of the little solace they had asleep in their tiny wooden cells.

Frank was the oldest at thirty-three, and without affirmation their leader. Grief blanketed them at the impending loss more than the drenching rain.

"I want every tenth one of you to step forward," said the second in charge. No one moved. He continued, "Well, the two of you select me twenty out of the crowd." Minutes went by as the two bosses pulled men out of the crowd.

They were pushed down to their knees one at a time. The pain of hitting the ground shocked even the deafest ear. The overseer then took out his whip and gave each of them twenty lashes. "This is for anyone who even thinks of getting any silly notion like Frank; no ears, no castration, just someone will be killed for payment, and we'll spread our joy amongst the women and children too. Go home now, or there'll be someone else who will pay."

Grumbling and mumbling ebbed as the crowds waned. All that was left was poor Frank strung up by his heels from the side of the barn with his shirt inverted over his face. His body was covered by blood and bruises; this was definitely not a testament for a fine man and worker.

Frank had turned a gin mill for personal use into a nationally known brand of whiskey; alas there was no credit to be given. His two poor little girls were taken in by a family member and the priestess. They might not ever know their parents or what they struggled for, hoped for, and possibly died too early for.

Day came and went, and all were forbidden to cut Frank down. Everyone thought he was dead as they continued about their business walking by their symbol of oppression and freedom; the next night he finally came to. The stable boy ran for help, and several released him. They brought salve and cloth for his wounds. After patching him up they gave him a horse and food to try to make it to the North and freedom.

Mr. Johnson never went out anymore, and slowly got worse as he drank more and more. When he eventually died two weeks later no one cared.

Mrs. Johnson was free. She went out and stayed out. She would have one of the white hands drive her because she didn't trust her property other than for menial tasks. She went to church daily, going to mass then attending lunch, meetings, and a late afternoon social. Then she would come home and go to bed, her own separate bed, straight away just as she had done for twenty years.

After the turmoil of Mr. Johnson's death, the few in charge decided that there was a price to be paid for Frank's escape. Again the men were brought out, and each asked to confess to stealing the horse and letting Frank go. No one responded. This time someone was shot.

Lucinda came out of her sleep or coma the same night Frank left. She got better, and spent many a night sneaking into the quarters on the other side just to see Mollie. Yet, she was happy to have Mary all to herself to ease her pain.

She took the scorn of her people on that side of camp. They were already apprehensive of taking orders from Frank because he was lighter, smarter, could read and write, and treated better. Frank was tall, strong, and fair, with long flowing white hair and beard, which was strange for his age. He stood up for them so they let the color thing go unspoken and only harbored slight ill feelings towards Frank and Lucinda Lampton. With the birth of Mollie, and Lucinda sleeping with Mr. Johnson, her side of the plantation ostracized her even more.

Years passed and things settled down as much as they could with the ugliness of slavery, civil strife, the Emancipation Proclamation, and the war. However, Frank was into the wind. Word got back that he had enlisted in the Union Troops across the state border. Happy that he might still be alive, she still lamented over the loss.

Mary and Mollie met for the first time just after their seventh birthday. It was a warm afternoon during the winter. Some grains were still tall and wavered in the afternoon's haze, blanketing the orange red sun setting over the glistening water. It was a lazy Sunday, the one day in the evening that most often got a time of rest.

Mary was sent to the well to get water, and Mollie was wandering through the fields looking for a place to lay and daydream. Mary had an old wooden bucket with a hole on one side. That was the only reason she was able to keep it. Her days were filled with ironing.

She would take a cast iron and put it in the fire until red hot and pull it out with a straw pad she made and covered with part of her tattered dress. While she ironed Mrs. Johnson's clothes, she would have another iron in the fire waiting to be used.

Mollie's life was a little easier. One of the boys would bring out the carpets and rugs every day, and she would beat them. Fifty-three rugs everyday she hit ridding them of dust and who knows.

Mary tripped over Mollie in the field spilling her water and tumbling onto the ground. Mary ranted, "What did you do that for? Why are you here? You better come up fighting 'cause I am."

"You scared the 'be-Jesus' out of me," screamed Mollie back at her. "You should have watched where you were going."

"Some of us have to work. That was the last of the well water. Now, I'll have to go all the way to the river through the back woods to get water for our supper. It will be dark soon, and I can't be caught out after dark or someone will steal me away."

As they both picked themselves up off the ground, their eyes met. There was some bonding as if they had known each other all of their lives. There was nothing but silence in response to the anger that had been brewing.

They touched each other's smudged face. Mary then grabbed a handful of hair. She had never seen anything like it. Here was someone of color with green, brown, and gray eyes and long wavy hair.

"Let go that hurts," said Mollie. "How would you like it if I grabbed your hair?" Seconds later she did just that.

"Ow," whined Mary. "Leave me be. I just wanted to see if your hair was real."

"Well it is, and from what I hear, so is yours. It's a lot fuller and coarser than mine, but see," as she yanked it again, "It is the same."

"Let's both let go on a count of three. One, two, three." They both let go, and then grabbed each other falling to ground. They wrestled and tumbled until each got tired. Neither struck a punch. As they lay on the ground, Mollie remarked, "Your eyes are the exact same color as mine. I've never seen anyone with all three colors in their eyes like us.

Mary said, "I don't care. Look what you've done to my only dress. I can't go home like this, especially without water; I'll get a beating."

"Go get your water then. You messed up my church dress. I won't be able to eat supper this dirty."

"You should get it for me. If it wasn't for you, then I would have never spilled it."

"I have some time since I won't be eating supper, and I'm bored. I'll go down to the river with you."

"I don't need you to go down with me. If you had more chores like I do, you wouldn't be bored."

"Don't you ever dream of getting away; doing something else; seeing exciting places; meeting a handsome man? Well, I do, and that's what I was doing on the ground; trying to figure out how to earn some brownie points."

"I know you house people just sit around, dress up and eat well, and are almost like the "Pilgrims" or "W's, you're owned by and favored by. Oh, that's right you are them with your good hair, small nose and lips, and corn husk faces."

"Well, who are you talking about with your dark face, big lips and nose, and woolly hair?"

"Your Mama had the nappy hair. Course I guess it fell out laying with old sorry Mr. Johnson."

"You take that back," as Mollie jumped on Mary and they tumbled down the hill towards the edge of the bayou. They continued to wrestle in the mud and pulling each other's hair until they heard the rustling of trees and bushes.

"It's a bear! We got to get out of here quick." That area of the woods became silent of birds, all types of critters, and even the buzz of mosquitoes as a large mouth opened with a growl. They nearly made it up the nearby tree when Mollie could feel a pinch on her big toe. The pain crept up her leg to her mouth and a loud anguishing yelp squealed out.

Mary screamed as she saw Mollie's blood as the bear continued to jump and paw at her. So, she lowered herself, broke off a limb, and tried to hit the bear on his nose. She whiffed on each of her three swipes. On the fourth swing she lost the footing of one foot, and the bear bit her toe, too.

Minerva moaned as she fell out of the huge chair on the dais, and Snowball stopped talking. George ran to her side to prop her up on the floor. She seemed to be all right physically other than being exhausted. Some of the others helped George get Minerva upstairs.

As the days went by Minerva got stronger and stronger. In one week she was off to the track again. This time I picked the three winners for her and she gave me a dollar. I brought a whole bag of "triple" popcorn for myself on the way home.

Our days and interactions got better. While out with Erna on errands, I heard her call my great-grandmother, Mother Adams, as Papa did. However, in Erna's broken English and German accent it sounded like one word, "MotherAdams." It stuck, and I did the same.

The second month things went smoother as we fell into a routine. Papa came in with a new idea again for stocks. He had the initial offering on an uranium mine, and put our name on each of the stocks.

His trial at the Supreme Court would be early fall. They discussed driving there in their '57 Bel Air. This was the car where I was always slow to get out of so that I could bounce up and down a few times on the back seat. Mother Adams was recovering, albeit slowly, so they thought it might be safe to try the séance again.

The Friday before the séance I went down to Papa's office to copy hundreds of papers for his impending trial in Washington. Papa was supposed to take me back home, but he never came. I called back to the house because I didn't feel comfortable enough to get on the "El" and bus by myself.

Mother Adams called me a cab, but told me to wait in the office until she had the night watchmen call me. Before he ever did, the police came rushing in with their guns drawn and screaming, "Arms behind your head and on the floor. Who are you? Where is he?"

I lay awfully still without responding. Minutes later after they went through the inner offices, one of the detectives realized my age. "Why don't you sit up, and tell us who you are?"

"I'm Attorney George C. Adams' great-granddaughter."

"Where is he? We came to pick him up?"

"I don't know; he was supposed to be here an hour ago to pick me up. Even my great-grandmother didn't know where he was when I called. But, he didn't do anything."

"That's not for you or us. We're here to bring him in. A gun registered to him was left at a murder scene."

The phone rang. I jumped towards it and one of the officers grabbed me. I spouted out, "It's just my cab. I want to go home."

The detective answered, "Yes?" Moments later he confirmed that's who the call was from by saying, "She's got a ride. You can go. I'll be taking her home, now."

"I'd rather go with the cabbie. That's who my great-grandmother arranged to come for me. He won't get paid."

"He won't mind to stay out of trouble. Let's go."

It was a long ride home down Lake Shore Drive. When I arrived my great-grandmother told me to go to my room. I started to turn, and one of the cops put his hand on my shoulder, "We still need her for questioning."

"I don't think so. She's a minor under my supervision. Most importantly, she has no information. Go child, and get ready for dinner." Mother Adams put her arm across my shoulders and walked me away from the policemen to my room. She closed the door behind me.

I could hear her go on, "Gentleman come in and have a seat."

"We prefer to stand. We have some questions for you."

She responded, "Suit yourself; I'm going to sit."

"Where's your husband?"

"As I told you over the phone, I don't know. This morning at breakfast, he said that he would bring our great-granddaughter home from work with him, and that should have been over an hour ago. I was just as surprised as she was when she called saying that he never showed up."

Their voices faded as they went into the living room against my best attempts to listen through the door. I showered and changed so that I would be ready to make my grand appearance as a sleuth.

Erna knocked on my door for dinner. At the table I didn't see Papa, and it was as quiet as if I had made a faux pas. Mother Adams asked Erna to bring her paper, pen, and a bowl of water. She wrote Papa's name down three times, put it flat in the bowl, poured sugar over it, and then the water. Next she got up from the table, put the bowl on the window sill, paced for a while, then wrote something else, placed it in another bowl and put it in the freezer. "That's what I did for that Camille woman and all of those Cicero hooligans." She continued moving about and brought back a crystal ball. She stared into it for twenty minutes without a word.

Erna and I went about clearing the dinner table. While back in the kitchen we heard a thump. We pushed through the swinging door to see Mother Adams slumped onto the table. We touched her, but no response.

"Great-grandmother! Are you all right? Erna, what should we do?"

Erna shrugged her shoulders, and sat Great-grandmother upright in her chair. "Let's see if this isn't one of her spells. We'll wait a few minutes."

Fifteen minutes further went by; probably making it a total of more than thirty minutes that Mother Adams was out. This was well past any time span that I had heard her or Papa mention, so I went to call an ambulance.

Erna came to the butler's pantry where the phone was, as I started to dial the "O" all the way around on the old black phone. She pushed my hand down onto the receiver. "No, child. It's too soon. Let's give her a little more time. She hasn't fallen out of the chair, so maybe means it's one of her spells."

Fifteen more minutes ticked by as the nervous sweat exuded on both our clothes as we stared at Mother Adams trying to get any indication of the severity of her health. "Where's Papa? I know he would know what to do. I saw him try smelling salts on her last spell out at the racetrack. Do you know if they have any in their room?"

"I think so. Stay with her, and I'll be right back."

In the short time that Erna had left us, I got an urge to rub my hands together and snap my fingers before saying, "At the count of three you will awake and remember everything that happened. One, two, three."

Nothing, and still Erna hadn't come back. I tried the same sequence only louder. For my third time I got up right on top of her, and tried as loudly as Papa had done before.

I jumped and fell back into the table as her eyes opened. I hugged her in exhilaration that she was okay, and the success of my attempts. There was no response from her.

"Great-grandmother, talk to me. What should I do? Wake up at the count of three, when I snap my fingers. One, two, three, wake up Minerva." Mother Adams woke up, I screamed, "Oh, my God!"

She started talking in the same voice that I heard down in the church last week. It was Snowball! He started narrating the tale of the slaves down in Kentucky again, exactly were he left off that Sunday.

The adrenalin and pain took over Mary. This time she landed a direct blow on the bear's nose. His mouth shut, and he fell to the ground. Mollie pulled her up, and they waited minutes crying, holding their bleeding nubs, and praying the bear would go back into the woods.

Mollie tore her skirt and gave Mary a strip to wrap her toes, which she in turn did for herself. Balling, the two of them side by side up a tree hanging on for dear life, while the other hand throbbed with blood seeping through each finger ringing the dinner bell for the myriad of creatures infesting the back woods.

The sun set and finally they heard the bear rustle bushes and run off heralding their chance for escape. Each tried to move with her wound, but it was awkward and terribly painful. They decided that in order to get back to the stables, something else had to be done. Mary tore her tattered skirt of burlap off at the bottom. She tied the strip to their legs, and they hopped and supported each other back through the field and woods as if they had a third leg.

"Where have you two been," asked the priestess as she spotted the two coming upon the plantation proper?

"Where does it look like we've been? Don't we smell like back woods," snapped Mollie overtaken by the aggravation and pain.

The priestess popped Mollie at the base of her neck. "I don't care how light or white you are. Better mind your elders, and speak civil when spoken to otherwise I'll get a switch."

"You're not my momma. Plus, I'm going to tell the boss what you did."

"Shush, your mouth! We've got enough trouble round here without you adding to it, or mouthing off. Get back to the big house with your fancy ways and clothes. Git," as the priestess was about to swat Mollie's behind!

Mary grabbed the priestess' hand mid-air saying, "She's hurt like I am. She saved me. Well, we saved each other from the bear. He bit both our toes, so we're blood related now. We need to get the mid-wife to tend us."

They hopped to the mid-wife's shanty. She was sitting waiting for her water. "What took you so long?"

"The bear got us," sniveled Mary.

"Miss Mollie don't you know that everyone is looking for you. Just when things have settled down a little bit, you two are going to stir them up."

"Here, let me look at your feet." She put a poultice on each of them and bound their toes with swaddling.

"Go, now; quickly before someone sees you two together." Mollie released the bindings on their two legs, and hopped on one leg to the back of the big house. Once there, she was lambasted by her older cousin.

"Where have you been? You should have been back here for dinner hours ago, and what happened to your church dress?"

"We were trapped up a tree by a bear. We couldn't get up fast enough, and he got each of our big toes. See!"

"Who's this 'We'?"

"Mary, the colored girl. You know she has the same eyes as me. After today, we're blood sisters, like the Indians."

"Don't you ever say that, and I definitely don't want you seeing her. They stay in their section, and we stay in ours."

"But, why?"

"That's just how it is, and because I say so. As long as you live under my roof you do as I say. You hear me?"

"I can't. She saved my life, and I saved her. I just got to see her."

"Smack, " and Mollie's face recoiled after the blow her cousin gave to her jaw. The tears rolled out as quickly as water from the pump. "And, if you don't shush, I'll give you something to cry about. You can go to bed without your supper. Now, go! Don't bring that girl up in this place ever again."

Chapter Four
"Who Has A Secret"

I went back home for the fall and curiously read and asked family members about Mother Adams, Minerva Lampton Young Adams, and Papa, George Cornelius Adams. The older generation said nothing, period. Just like, "No, n-o-e, no;" evoked that proverbial silence. Every now and then you would get bits and pieces of the story if you caught one of the aunts or uncles alone, otherwise you got that scowl from one end of the table's two book-ends, George and Minerva. I still needed to find out about the slave days of their parents and how they got their land and money.

My intrigue was piqued at one Sunday dinner which fell on a holiday after a funeral earlier that week for someone the older generation knew which brought about funny and sarcastic comments about growing up with gamblers always around. This was a first of anything, and now some juicy gossip. They joked about how my grandmother got in the ice-box to hide during a raid and her coat tail sticking out gave her away; my uncle going down a coal chute because of associates that peddled their wares outside their house; and some of the unsavory characters whom my great-grandfather defended that would stop by. That was the curse of having some money and owning a very large house on the "strip," the same block with all of the action from the Savoy Ballroom and Regal Theatre; notwithstanding the fact that they were doing business as a well known defender and psychic.

Family continued to remark about the numbers runner with his slips of paper that had his "stand" outside the house, Mr.'s Sym's, and a candy stand down the street. One quip was about one of Jones' lieutenants that stayed in a room that they let out in the basement or lower floor, which also elicited memories of sawdust, a policy wheel, and lots of money on tables. The police who knew my family well would go through the motions of searching through the house looking for him, but to no avail. They also told about earlier days and the Jones Brothers, who were considered one of Chicago's biggest gambling syndicates.

The Jones Brothers: Edward, George, McKissic were family friends through my great-grandfather who was an alumnus from Howard like Ed. Papa also frequented Ed's tailor shop at 43d and Indiana. It was "Big Ed," until the attempt on his life prompting a move to Mexico, who got psychic or spiritual information from my great-grandmother. Rumor had it that he would often comment on the advice that he got from his spiritualist on 47th St., "Rev. M. J. Adams, Metaphysician, Teacher, and Healer," who moved to Chicago in the 1880's and later bringing her parents, her sister Susie, and her grandmother Sucky Campbell who died in Chicago in 1891 at 84. Ed would get his daily reading and numbers from her, and she played the same numbers. The story I was told was that this is how "4-11-44" became the number not to hit because Reverend Adams said that it would bring disaster. Subsequently these numbers hit; Mother Adams later foretold that these numbers would hit two days in a row. According to the *Chicago Tribune*, "4-11-44," came in on February 5, 1898, paying $3,000 each. (*Tribune*, 1898)

The biggest family mystery was about, who at the time I thought was my grandfather's brother, Samuel E. Young, born 1872 in Chattanooga, Tennessee. Sam came to Chicago around 1896 and worked as a porter for the Windermere Hotel in Hyde Park where Henry "Teenan" Jones ran a gambling house. "Teenan" also operated two other gambling houses in Hyde Park, the Chicago Beach Hotel for Blacks, and the nicer white only place, the Lakeside Club.

"'Teenan' Jones was one of the first saloon and gambling operators to open outside 'Whiskey Row' downtown on Harrison and State Streets which was controlled by John 'Mushmouth' Johnson. In 1903, Mayor Carter Harrison revoked the license of Johnson's saloon on 'Whiskey Row' because the City's 'Graft Committee' collected evidence that it was impossible to win at Johnson's gambling games, and if anyone did, they were soon parted with their money one way or the other before the evening was out." (Spear, p. 77)

"From 1896 to 1903 the Lone Star Saloon and Palm Garden were operating in what was known as Whiskey Row on State and

Harrison streets. A small bartender would often sell to unsuspecting customers his 'special drink' which consisted of raw alcohol and other unidentified powders that would put him in an unconscious state. The bartender would then rob the victim and dump him in an alley near the tavern. The name of the bartender? Mickey Finn, of course. Even though Mr. Finn gave payoffs to the local police, the tavern was closed down by them on 16 December 1903. Mr. Finn did return to bartend and was known to sell his 'formula' to others." (http://en.wikipedia.org/, 2011)

A "Mickey Finn," is what was believed aided in the kidnapping and death of my great-grandfather thinking he was "Policy Sam," who made Chicago's policy a million dollar business. Sam died on December 2, 1902, in the middle of the night in an alley at the back of a building on Monroe. The only thing close was the Chicago and Northwestern (C&NW) or Madison Street Station at Canal and Madison east of the alley. "For many years, C&NW jointly operated west coast trains with Union Pacific and Southern Pacific. In addition to intercity trains, C&NW operated an extensive commuter service on its North, Northwest and West lines." (http://www.dhke.com/ 2011)

Samuel did not live in the vicinity where he died. The location was not in the direction he would go to get to his home in Hyde Park on the Southside in Ward 7, and all commuter trains headed North or West from this depot. It was also about 12 blocks northwest of his job at Siegel, Cooper & Co. which was not open at this time, and past the river, which was not the area to stroll in. The "S & C" department store was two blocks north of where he had met my great-grandmother coming out of The Fair at State and Adams where she was a "Bath Attendant [at a] department store," according to one of the two different listings in the 1910 Census (one with parents in one house and one with son in another house).

There were plenty of saloons like Finn's for drinking which could have wreaked havoc on Sam's kidneys, and of course, the gambling, as well as the brothels and bordellos of the "Levee," or "Red Light District" which were nearby and open at this time of the morning, might have added to his troubles. Although, the "Levee" had been moved farther south in 1890 to: State to Clark from 19th to 22nd Streets, several independents remained in the original location at the saloons and halls from Dearborn to Clark and Harrison to Polk Streets. There was no reason given for Samuel E. being in the alley of Monroe and Clinton on a very cold early Tuesday morning.

It was a shame to be treated for something you didn't do and for someone who you were mistaken for. The tale was that our Samuel E. Young was drugged and kidnapped because he was often confused with the other Samuel Young, or "Policy Sam." They both were colored porters from Tennessee; married someone from Kentucky; had similar complexions, body builds, and according to one census were less than one year apart in age; and lived on South 29th Street at one point.

To fuel this theory, if one looked at the two Samuel Youngs from the census you see only two blacks with that name. The Sam Young, who appears to be "Policy Sam," as relayed by the University of Kentucky website was born in 1868 in Alabama. (http://www.uky.edu/, 2011) However, Ron Chepesiuk in *Black Gangsters of Chicago* has "Policy Sam" born in 1858 in Alabama marrying an Alma Miller in Louisville before moving to Chicago and having nine children.

Strangely enough in the 1900 U. S. Census, you find a Sam Young (Jan. 1865) from Tennessee married to a Lucy Young of North Carolina (Feb. 1875) married in 1894 with six kids on 3133 S. Dearborn as a "Gambler." The 1910 Census shows Samuel Young on 29th & Dearborn at age 42 married to Ada [Johnson] Young, and a 1930 Census has a Sam Young, 57 (born 1873) is widowed as a "Bondsman" on 3135 S. Rhodes living with an Albert Johnson.

At first I thought my great-grandfather might be one and the same as "Policy Sam," because it was reported that after a certain period, around the time my great-grandfather was found dead, no one really saw "Policy Sam." He was reported on the census by friends, and others kept the tale going that he had just left or would be back soon. There were reports of him being here, there, and everywhere.

R. M. Lombardo cites the *Chicago Defender* and the Illinois Writer's Project in his work, *Black Mafia: African American Organized Crime In Chicago 1890-1960*, that, "Three men are credited with bringing policy to Chicago, a white man named Patsy King, an oriental named 'King Foo' and Sam Young, a black. Patsy King, who owned the Bucket Shop Saloon, was believed to be a Mississippi riverboat gambler who had migrated to Chicago at the time of the 1893 World's Fair. King was reportedly the genius gambler who invented his own games of chance and had grown rich on the proceeds. He reportedly gave the idea for policy to a porter in his saloon named Sam Young. With the financial backing of King, Young opened a small policy wheel in downtown Chicago." Lombardo then cites Drake and Clayton that, "John 'Mushmouth' Johnson was probably the first important gambler to see the potential of policy. Johnson entered the policy racket during the late 1890's in partnership with Patsy King and King Foo." This probably led to the intimidation of Sam to join the others or quit the business.

Nathan Thompson states in his book, *"Kings" - The True Story of Chicago's Policy Kings and Numbers Racketeer*s:

> Like most Americans, Chicagoans lost confidence in the Republican Party's ability to govern, thus setting the stage for a major shift of power in the political arena and a subsequent shift of power over the politically protected Policy racket. When the smoke cleared, one up-and-coming soldier in the regular Democratic organization would emerge as the driving force behind the historic swinging of the Black vote. He too would emerge as the man who would transform Policy Sam's nickel and dime, street corner hustle into a mega-million dollar industry: the always charming, fast-talking, well-connected, mostly frugal Ed Jones. . .The Jones brothers ran a Policy station from the rear of their Jones Brothers Tailor Shop at 4312 South Indiana Avenue. (2007)

Of course, if someone was trying to kill you, one of the most infamous gambling operators known as the "Policy King" in Chicago that made millions and snubbed the white gangsters and politicians, this could be a great opportunity for Samuel R. Young to disappear even before the anti-policy legislation passed by Congressman Ed Green in 1905. (Lombardo, p. 47) "Policy Sam" left the numbers game and went underground at this time.

"In 1915, Young reentered the game introducing policy gambling along South State Street in the black community. His betting slips bore the name 'policy' and he was his own 'runner' (collector of bets). A waitress from the Pullman Restaurant at 31st and State reportedly pulled the numbers out of his derby hat while standing under the elevated train station at that location. Sam Young is remembered as the 'father of the game.'" (Ill. Writer's Project)

The two Youngs' lives continued to parallel even though one was dead. In December 21, 1928, "Four bandits, two of whom were said to be white, early Sunday morning invaded the home of Mrs. Elia Morphis, 4536 Calumet Ave., where a card party was in progress, shot and slightly wounded two men, held up the other nine guests and escaped with $175 taken from Sam Young." (*Chicago Defender*, 1928, p. 5)

Our Sam's widow and son lived at 4523 S. Calumet which was right across the street. Also Samuel E. Young's daughter-in law belonged to the group that held the Bridge Parties, or card parties. Lucille Young was mentioned in the *Chicago Defender* on more than one occasion throwing a card party for the neighborhood group.

Still no one talked about Sam. So, I started my probing on George C. Adams.

Chapter Five
"Fiction or Non-Fiction"

Every Sunday or holiday I tried to get more information on family, genealogy, and why my family was said to have started the Cicero Riot in 1951. Finally I overheard some family members talking. It was a piecemealed story about my great-grandfather. Papa never told his story, and no documentation was offered.

The story started with, "We heard that he was the great-grandson of President John Quincy Adams," who was most noted for his eloquent defense of the slaves in the historic Amistad Case and being the sole cause for the U. S. House's "Gag Rule." To my understanding, an Adams family friend had traveled from Paris to visit with the Adams family in Massachusetts after having met President Adams as a child at a reception for him in London. Tales of numerous opportunities had been conveyed convincing Mr. Williams to move to America to extend his business. Shortly afterwards his wife and her servant, Viola, and her daughter Henrietta made the crossing.

Later that year Charles Adams was elected to the U. S. House of Representatives in 1858. To break up the long trip from Massachusetts to Louisiana as winter approached, the Williams took advantage of an invitation to visit with Charles and his brother Henry and be guests of the Buchannan's at the White House in 1858. The parties and tales of Europe, books read, and the pleasure of drink made the family including their servants the life of the parties. The two younger men similar in interests and temperaments became fast friends.

Henrietta was a huge success because no one was sure of her parentage, but everyone knew her parents white. Her features were almost indistinguishable as being of African descent, and because the Williams let her dress the part as the daughter they didn't have (or did they?) she fit well into society speaking three languages, playing the piano, and being well versed in literature, business, and politics. Williams left the women of the family in the D. C. area while he purchased thousands of acres of property northeast of Baton Rouge. He stayed with friends in New Orleans while his mansion was being built on his new plantation. After things got settled he purchased a house in New Orleans and brought his wife and Viola there.

Henrietta was invited to stay at the White House once the Williams left as a tutor. A few months later Henrietta started to show and gossip spread around the White House. Henrietta was pregnant, with no father, no man of her own, no mother around, and now ostracized because of innuendo that the baby was possibly the President's son's.

Henrietta cried and cried as she was no longer welcome in the main house and restricted to the servants' quarters out back. She wrote to her mother and Mrs. Williams, and she was sent for to have the child, Charles, born December of 1860, at the home of another member of the Williams family. After a few months Henrietta was requested back to the White House to finish her tutoring while Charles stayed with the Williams in New Orleans.

In 1860, Mrs. Williams had a boy, which was a surprise to everyone because of its possibility. Henrietta continued on in the employ of the President until she became pregnant again. This was through the Lincoln administration and up until the time that Charles Adams suddenly left to be Lincoln's Ambassador to Britain in 1861. Henrietta went back to Louisiana and stayed until she had her second child, who died in stillbirth.

All this was too much for Henrietta and she started showing too much affection for little Charles, and Mrs. Williams became quite irate and crazed. Henrietta was sent to the plantation in northeastern Louisiana with her mother. In 1872, her mother became sick and died of consumption a few months later.

Charles left New Orleans at thirteen and joined his mother; later meeting and marrying Violet Gibson in 1882 in the same area of Rayville, LA. Violet was born August 30, 1858, in Mabel, Louisiana to George Stious from Virginia and a Native American of the Choctaw Nation whose land Mr. Williams owned. Shortly afterwards they had their first child Frank in 1883. Then George came in 1884, then Minnie in 1891, Oscar in 1894, and Orcy in 1898.

Not too long afterward some civil servant stopped by and presented separate papers for Violet and Charles. One stated that he and his mother years ago had been signed over to the Choctaw Tribe as Freedman by Mrs. Williams and had to leave for Oklahoma. The other stated that as a "half-breed" Violet had to go, too.

I could not find the family listed in the optional Dawes Rolls:

> Officially known as The Final Rolls of the Citizens and Freedmen of the Five Civilized Tribes in Indian Territory, the Dawes Rolls list individuals who chose to enroll and were approved for membership in the Five Civilized Tribes (Cherokee, Chickasaw, Choctaw, Creek, and Seminole.) Enrollment for the Dawes Rolls began in 1898 and ended in 1906. In most cases the ages indicated on the rolls are the age of individuals around 1902. . .
>
> Tribal association will be listed as 'By Blood,' 'Intermarriage,' or 'Freedmen.' Intermarriage indicates the person was married to a citizen of the tribe. You may also see the letters 'I W' for Intermarried White. Freedmen were the former slaves of the Five Civilized Tribes and their descendants. (http://www.okhistory.org, 2011)

The forced migration of the Adams family from Louisiana to Oklahoma sounds plausible. It was too much to believe that Papa was the great-grandson of President John Quincy Adams. Then I read that Camille claimed he was the grandson of Pres. Adams in her book, which was good fodder for family jokes.

The town of Rayville in Richmond Parrish, Louisiana is noted for its Creoles, and Mrs. De Rose stated that this was Papa's claim to be French and Indian. (Rose, 1953) According to another website, "French Creoles:"

> The Choctaw of Louisiana are the most widely dispersed group, the East Baton Rouge Parish community representing principally mixed-blood Choctaw descendants now living in an urban setting. The other relict Choctaw groups represent eighteenth-century bands that moved into the present state under Spanish dominion.
>
> The largest contemporary Choctaw populations are descended from eighteenth-century Choctaw settlements in Rapides Parish and on the Ouachita River. These groups now compose the Jena Band of Choctaw and another, unrelated group, the Clifton community. In 1903 some of the Louisiana Choctaw joined members of their tribe living in Oklahoma. (http://www.frenchcreoles.com, 2011)

"NO, N-O-E, NO" - THE CICERO RIOT STORY

This is the story I believed while growing up. No one offered any other information and I could not find any documentation in my forays into old pictures, news clippings, or family records at the time.

Chapter Six
"Facts, Nothing But The Facts"

Finally during Easter dinner I was able to maneuver my way onto the first kids' card table in the dining room because of an illness from one of the table's regulars. Someone from the main table mentioned that they think they saw Camille De Rose on 52nd & Drexel. Vaguely I remember seeing a book with the name when I put all of the family books into the many bookcases we had in the basement after our move from 68th and Dante to 97th and LaSalle on the far Southside of Chicago. I lunged for the topic again like diving into a pond that you didn't know the depth of, "What happened during the 'Cicero Riot'?" A fork dropped, then came a throat clearing, and then the awful hush.

There it was, our dirty family secret! I always wondered why my father and great-grandfather never really fraternized more than just being cordial. I saw pictures of them together in my great-grandfather's office and knew Papa stood up for Dad in their wedding in 1948. Also, I didn't understand why my father a National Honor Society and MENSA member was kicked out of Law School because of bad grades. Why my father's father was on the cornerstone in a small Polish town north of Chicago and he was a member of an elite fraternity of wealthy, collegiate African American men, but he had no degree, and we lived modestly. Something didn't make sense.

Dad lowered his head, and Papa glared. No one answered but I got a quick kick in the shin from my older sister by ten years. Back at home, I went downstairs while everyone was asleep and my father was out on his second job. There was the book, *The Camille De Rose Story*, in its black, red, and white cover. I'm sure that it was planned that way; just as she put on the cover, "The True Story of the Cicero Race Riots...Admittedly, the riots were planned and provoked." It was published by the Camille De Rose Publishing Company in 1953.

In the forward, Camille De Rose wrote, "The explosive elements were: (a) the ever present race repellants, real, and imagined; (b) a town without colored citizens and colored citizens without living quarters, and (c) a group of colored incendiaries on the prowl for a chance to light a fuse." (p. 2) "The building, 6139-42 W. 19th St., Cicero, IL became the center of a racial war, of a planned insurrection." (p. 1)

Ms. De Rose claims that she originally just came to hear my great-grandfather speak at the "Property Owners League" that met near his office in downtown Chicago. Subsequently, he published a "Cicero Resolution for Rent De-control" in his newspaper, The *Chicago Free Enterprise*. As a result, she sought legal advice from Papa and that their initial meetings were not on the discussion of having Negro tenants, but to her recollection she called him about questions of "Rent Control." She finally went down to his office to meet the attorney of her dreams.

He was, "A Negro Attorney, his name is George C. Adams, with an office in the Chicago Loop. I met him by accident. . . I did not have the slightest notion that he was a Negro. If his complexion is of a dark texture, it was as light if not lighter than many white men. His features were that of a white man." (p. 96)

"He said that he was 62 years old, 32 years as a lawyer, and that he was 'Creole' or French & Indian, and that he was a grandson of John Quincy Adams, and that he played in the White House when a child; that he served during the second world war on the peace time draft, located in Washington, D. C., where he personally knew the late President Roosevelt." (p. 110) She also commented that, "Attorney Adams said that he owned an insurance company, his own newspaper, and large real estate holdings." (p. 110)

It was three o'clock in the morning and I needed to get to bed, but I got to the part were, Mrs. De Rose said she had a, "Short but consuming romance with a Negro." (p. 14) Oh, my! Papa was having an affair with her, which meant he lied to Mom. I immediately turned to the book cover jacket to stare at her picture. My small flashlight did her no justice. I was aghast! I kept reading.

How could this be? I know Papa was married, and her salutation was Mrs. It was now six o'clock in the morning. I could hear my mother's alarm clock which meant soon my father would be back from the graveyard shift and I would get a spanking with his belt, the ironing cord, or his shaving strap (in worsening severity). I hustled upstairs barely escaping.

The next night I was back in the lower level. In the meetings and calls that followed Mrs. De Rose became dependant upon my great-grandfather. If not down at his office everyday she was on the phone to him several times a day. It wasn't until months after her involvement with him professionally, and the involvement she imagined personally in her head that she had realized that he was a Negro. If not for my father, great-grandmother, and other associates, she would have continued to think him white and propagate the fantasy in her mind. Camille wrote that her, "Mindfulness of race distinction brought her closely to marriage with a Negro attorney...I merely wish to say that this attorney became identified with the restoration of my building, as I hoped, and therefore with my very soul." (p. 16) Alas, to show her warped sense of reality and propriety, both Negro attorneys she was infatuated with, Adams initially then Keys, had features that were night and day apart. The only two things in common besides knowing her were that both were African-American attorneys, and both were married before and after meeting her.

As time went on she changed her outlook on Papa. Meeting one's family, especially, wife, and finding out that he was colored put the brakes on even in someone groping for love and security. "Adams bless him, took over the building and with it my guilt as a violator, my hostile tenants and a thousand and one worries." (p. 137)

As she had innumerably repeated, "I fled for my life! Into the shelter of an elderly Attorney At Law, a man of learning, a member of a profession bound by its ethics. At this point in my story, I felt a great relief in having myself separated from my building, and from thousands of dollars worth of furniture. Now the burden shifted to Attorney Adams, under whose advice I went on. He was a lawyer. He could assert his rights. He explained that the 'persecution' of which he relieved me, and to which I had been unaccustomed, was the steady lot of the Negro; and it seems, or so he inferred, that in addition to the unspecial persecution which he endures as a citizen of 'mixed' ancestry." (p. 138) If not for Papa's associates of all races Camille probably would have never known he was Black, as she states in her book is what first alerted her to the fact that he might be colored.

My older sister who I shared a room with because she was back from college for spring break woke up one night as I was sneaking back to bed. She added that she had heard of Mrs. De Rose in later years. She affirmed the fact that back in the early fifties that months went by with Mrs. De Rose's usual appearances in and out of Papas' office downtown, or at the house at 4757 South Parkway, and her calling over to both of our houses late into the night. Everyone knew her by name. As she became more and more attached and dependent upon Papa, he started taking her out of the office. The only safe place became in public at lunch. My sister overheard an argument over the attention Papa paid Mrs. De Rose after one of her late calls when she stayed overnight at our great-grandparents'. Later she noticed a piece of paper with her name in the freezer.

As I continued to read I found out that Papa taking her out in public was the first of her complaints against Papa. He had people of all colors around him. Not because she was prejudice; she was not color-minded at all. She did observe among her many observations that everyone else thought of color as opposed to people just being people.

Nights went by as I continued to read, some times re-reading. I was running out of time. It was almost summer, and I would no longer have access to the book. Middle of the night reading on explosive items and family secrets were hard to comprehend and made for sleepless nights. Several key items as I read and made notes on, stuck out:

> Adams and Edwards are inseparable. Edwards is a silent partner in the literal sense of the word. He rarely spoke. As I said earlier, they look alike and act alike excepting that Adams talked for both. Edwards was introduced to me as the real estate agent, and, at least at the outset, they addressed each other as Mr. Adams and Mr. Edwards, unusual among office and business associates. Adams claimed that he never had any children. During the riots, the newspapers described Edwards as Adam's grand nephew-in-law! What does this contradiction signify? Whatever it signifies, it is a contradiction and puzzling. (p. 200)

Camille went on to say:

He then said that he had two buildings, clear of mortgages, each of value of $50,000 or $55,000; that he had thought of selling both and buying a larger building. (p. 129)

March 20, 1951, I signed an assignment to Mr. Adams of my beneficial interest to the title of my building. . .

When I later saw the document I noticed the name of Jewel Young. I asked who Jewel Young was. He said that Jewel Young was his wife's maiden name, and that it would be better not to let anyone know who had purchased the building. . . . He said that he would move into the building. I called to his attention the objection to colored people in Cicero. He said that neither his wife nor he could be identified as colored, and called my attention to the fact that he is generally regarded as white. He also said that even if they learned that he was 'mixed' that while they might show some resentment at first that they soon would become friendly and exchange courtesies. That had happened before. He had moved into white neighborhoods and had that experience. (p. 131)

The first time the Clarks tried to move into the Cicero apartment was June 8th, 1951. Camille cites my father's affidavit, which prompted me to stop again to see if I could find such supporting documents. I could not find anything that was not locked up. So I was off to bed again. I was becoming more and more anxious to find out what really happened so I broached the subject with my mother. She said that was a long time ago mid-stirring our dinner. She never stopped or continued the conversation.

It's strange to read about someone else's thoughts and opinions on your father and great-grandfather. You tend to think of them only in your familial way but they exist in different spheres and arenas, and that façade is something you can't see from the inside out. It only works in reverse.

I had two nights to go before I was shipped off to my great-grandparents again for the summer. I had to get enough info to pose intelligent probing questions to my great-grandfather because everything hinged on pleading your case logically, even just trying to go out. I learned to use his words: "Ergo," "Logically surmise," "Stands to reason," quickly.

Camille continued:

The second time on July 10th, they [Adams, Edwards, Clarks, Scotts] were met by a small crowd so they turned around so as not to endanger their children. They soon left the apartment, carefully locking the doors, and returned to the home of the Edwards on the South Side of Chicago.

The next day it was announced that the Clarks would try a third time. This time the word spread and almost 5,000 people were out. It started by kids throwing rocks, then fire, and screaming, "'We don't want niggers here,' and 'Throw Judge Barnes out.'" (p. 180)

They finally moved their furniture in at 10 am; 60 Cook County Sheriffs came out earlier before the requested National Guard ordered by Gov. Stevenson didn't start arriving until 1030 pm when the police line was broken. . .

By 930 pm the eight police deputies and six sheriffs men had arrested no one while the building burned down. By the end at 230 am, 19 were injured and 70 arrested. . .

Crowds re-assembled on the 13th but there were only minor happenings. . .

The decision to go it alone by the Clarks or by the lawyers that represent them, aided and abetted by the lawyer-weasel Adams, had vicious implications, of which I shall speak later. (p. 225)

They [Keyes & Leighton] who devoted their lives to the redemption of the Negro in his civil rights would not let me down, a white woman, caught in the tentacles of a Negro swindler [Adams]. (p. 232)

When later I appeared before the Grand Jury which investigated before the riots, I heard the clerk call out the name of Jewel Young. An infirmed childlike underdeveloped young lady arose in response to that name. Mrs. Adams adjusted the girl's hair. Apparently Jewel Yong was brought in response to a subpoena when her name was found in the record as the person to who the property was assigned. A feeling of pity gripped the jurors and she was asked but a few questions. This Jewel Young is not Adam's wife, of course, but as I was later informed, is a step daughter of a previous marriage. (p. 236)

Wow, another night. The more I read I became incensed. Every opportunity she had was now a negative about the family. She had nothing to do with any of them at this point and they were the culprits behind the Cicero Riot and her downfall. Her savior turned into the devil.

I was to leave the day after tomorrow, and this was my last night. I felt vindicated on behalf of my family when I read how her trouble continued after bringing so much to mine. She was arrested for carrying a gun in court, and after threatening my great-grandfather, my father, and my aunt Jewell. Later she was, "Committed to a mental institute in Kankakee, IL on June 30, 1952." (p. 288)

The psychiatrist who examined Ms. De Rose made the following statement, "'As she unfolded her story, it became increasingly apparent that emotional instability had been operative in her personality long before her involvement in litigation began. The continuous series of litigations that she has been involved in for the past few years had brought about still another unhealthy feature in her make-up; namely she had become distinctly paranoid in ideation and behavior. This paranoid feature spells danger for people she considers as her prosecutors.'" (p. 288) Doctor Harvey's letter to Judge Crowley helped a panel declare her insane on July 5, 1952.

Camille went on saying:

Every American should take a keen interest in that manifesto [NAACP 'Guidepost to Freedom'], for it may be the key to the threatening world war between the white and colored people. (p. 299)

It is folly to argue that the NAACP movement is presently too feeble to carry out its 'militant' program... We must not wait until the 'moment' attains momentum to be a menace, which most surely will engulf all citizens. (p. 300)

I had employed Attorney George C. Adams for the simple purpose of advising me on rent control questions, so that I may strictly comply with all rules and laws. He led me into violation, then advised me to place a $65,000.00 mortgage on my building, then to place the title to the building in a trust, then to assign the trust to him, then to invest my mortgage money in fake oil stock and other swindles; then to destroy my building in race riots planned by him and confederates. (p. 301)

Although Mr. Adams, besides being a lawyer and what not, is also a detective and clairvoyant and his wife a fortune teller, it wasn't the crystal ball that told him, 'there won't be any conviction.' (p. 310)

We can point to the so-called 'Cicero Race Riots.' Those riots were deliberately planned by Attorney Adams and followed through by the NAACP. Negroes and Orientals are not new to Cicero. Had Harvey Clark truly intended to live in my building, he might have moved into it quietly, as I said before... But such was not the intention at all. The NAACP membership had been dwindling and their leaders were hard put for an occasion to support a drive for funds and memberships. At the same time Attorney Adams found a situation which he could maneuver to support claims and lawsuits. He therefore staged a Roman holiday for entry of the Clarks and Adams to take over in Cicero. (p. 319)

Therefore the scheme of 'moving' the Clark's to Cicero was to keep the Clark's and others on the South Side. It did more! It whipped up excitement about 'civil rights,' discrimination, and race hatred... The plan worked so good for the NAACP that other rival groups rushed in to get some of the flood of gold. It also gave support for a lawsuit against the town of Cicero for $200,000. In other words the riots paid off. (p. 322)

Our laws and public opinion are sufficient to protect us against discrimination. Time will take care of the rest. The NAACP merely keeps alive race differences in the public mind. (p. 329)

The colored people are being 'sold down the river' by their own emotions whipped up by a group of lawyer-politicians, who exaggerate the prejudice of their white neighbors. They are still playing 'Uncle Tom's Cabin.' (p. 329)

It was amazing to me that not knowing anything about African Americans Mrs. De Rose now became an expert in her summations. She had to let the world know about her woes of allegedly: (1) being swindled by my family, (2) then my family swindling the public, and (3) the NAACP and all lawyers, taking advantage of the colored race and especially her. It was the "United States vs. Camille de Rose." (p. 138)

I wanted to read the end of her book and find out its outcome but sadly my last day of reading was cut short. It really turned into my last reading because my father came home early that night waiting for a storm to pass whilst repairing the street lights.

I was in trouble. I thought I would surely pay with some corporal punishment but he just told me, "Go to your room; you're on punishment. I'll talk to your mother when she gets up and decide what to do with you."

He looked hurt, "Stay out of things that are not yours. How would you feel if I went through your journal or diary?"

"It would hurt," as I hung my head. Before I turned to walk away I said, "It was a book in the bookshelf in the library, amongst all of the hundreds of books we have. I promise I didn't go through your things."

"I'm too tired; just go to your room. I don't want to have to take my belt off."

You could definitely see how disappointed he was of me, which was punishment enough. I whimpered off slowly, and he said, "Now." I ran, and we never spoke about the incident again.

The summer of 1966 went relatively well until Dr. King came to town to help out the Chicago Freedom Movement which was trying to emphasize Northern racial inequality especially in housing and public schools. I heard that King was planning to march through Cicero and I wanted to be there to see, especially in light of my family. Extra police and guards were called out because no one wanted what happened in 1951 to happen again. Now, I understand why my father was more upset then usual. He even skipped all of the Sunday brunches during this time period to avoid my great-grandfather and the topic.

On Friday, August 5th, I was determined to sneak away to join King. I packed a sandwich and a piece of fruit in a brown bag and almost made it out when my great-grandmother who I thought had left asked, "Where are you off to?"

"I'm off to march with Rev. King; we all have to do our part."

"Better march yourself right back in here."

"But, why? I owe it to our people and civil rights."

"No, you don't. We paid your debt and your children's debt. We, your family, have crusaded, fought, and died for the American way. We have given so much; we have had enough of Cicero. Go sit at the table and eat your lunch in peace. You don't have to be sold or separated from your family; you don't have to be forced to lay with some man because you're his property; you don't even have to marry because you can go to school, vote, buy property."

I did as I was told. Later I found out that King was persuaded to not march in Cicero but only in the Marquette and Gage areas. Some said it was too dangerous. Finally an agreement was worked out with Mayor Daley and the Chicago Real Estate Board. As usual nothing changed in Chicago.

Chapter Seven
"Business As Usual"

I pondered over the notes that I made from Camille De Rose's *The Cicero Riot Story*. Some of my writing was illegible due to my night reading and writing by flashlight.

One of the few things that Camille said which was not, "colored" by her tale of woe was that, "The Cicero Riots, brought world notoriety to a town which was not exactly a virgin in the news beforehand. The riots also brought to the forefront a specie of a 'cold war' which had simmered between the colored and the white population. It also turned the spotlight on subversive police methods, on the tug-and-pull of political cross-currents and on the amazing action and reaction of the courts." (p. 7) Even in her warped confusion she could see the systematic and institutional racism that cut many ways and could turn on anyone associated with persons of color, including her.

She continued her observations on the next page, "The building [6139-42 W. 19th St., Cicero, IL] became the center of a racial war, of a planned insurrection, and the town of Cicero, its police and town officials as well as Camille De Rose, were swept into the vortex of turmoil. The war brought the State militia to the rescue of the citizens, but it destroyed the 'empire' that I built. It also destroyed the myth of equality before the law; it swept aside the already tattered curtain of respectability which draped official and political corruption. There were tons of newsprint paper devoted to the riots and what followed in their wake, but the true story of the cause of the riots and their important incidents before, during, and after, never thus far came to light. These I relate in the ensuing pages, without 'color added,' and without reserve." (p. 8)

However, being associated with people of color and facing some of their issues in America, today much less in the 1950's before Civil Rights, is never what it appears. Color, hatred, and bigotry run deep. I'm sure she and others could sympathize, but when things got too tough they could get a pass or just disassociate. Just as Cicero's officials told her that she could come back home on more than one occasion. Even the Police Chief intimated that everything could be set right, "Come home." (p. 228) On the other hand, you can't just stop being Black.

Not only did Ms. De Rose have rent control and tenant issues she had financial and personal troubles. Her book jacket professes that, "In these pages of her book you will follow her through underworld haunts, jails, asylums, interracial loves, and soul stirring suicide attempts." Strangely enough a former prostitute with emotional problems and an arrest record had more credibility to a town and judicial system than two educated, professional men who had no psychological issues or criminal records. Oh, but they were, "Negroes." She laments that, "I should have known that it is dangerous to befriend or tolerate a Negro. . . Who is to blame for my miseducation? Yet I realize that the Negro incident would never have happened if the Cicero officials had not misled, not me but my lawyers, with their rent resolution."(p. 198)

My great-grandfather offered her a solution to one problem by buying her building, as he had done with many buildings, as did my father. At the time when she first met my great-grandfather in February of 1951, he owned two buildings in which he and family would stay, and my father's company owned a couple that they would flip or rent out.

My father's records show that on March 20, 1951, she assigned her property title and interest to George C. Adams. Early April Mrs. De Rose signed a statement which gave the building to Papa saying she would not bring Negroes into Cicero. Conversely, Mrs. De Rose attests to the Illinois Racial Commission that, "On account of the above condition, [rent control] I arranged to sell my furniture and lease my apartment to Mr. Charles Edwards who is a World War II veteran with an honorable discharge, a law student, his wife and his baby. He has been engaged in the real estate business for sometime. He and his wife are decent, respectable persons, and well educated. They would add dignity and credit to any neighborhood in which they lived." (p. 139)

That same week Mrs. De Rose states in her book, "On the last Sunday in March 1951, Adams called bringing with him a Negro man, wife, and sister whom he introduced as Mr. & Mrs. Edwards [my parents] – and mentioned the name of the other woman [my father's sister, Tessie] which I missed. Mr. Edwards was noticeably like Adams in features, height, and mannerisms, although of darker skin. Edwards acted impersonally; they spoke to each other as Mr. Edwards and Mr. Adams. . .had to steel myself to the occasion. . .He said Edwards was a smart real estate man and could take care of the building." (p. 139)

My father did take care of the building by collecting rent, letting apartments, and managing the building, such as securing insurance. The arrangement was set up through Camille De Rose's lawyer, his wife's grandfather. Dad was the owner and managing partner, real estate broker, and insurance broker of his two people company, Illinois Realty located at 3458 S. State St., Chicago, Ill.

His company leased space in the Binga Building at one of the two epicenters of Bronzeville, and my family lived on the same block as the other one. According to WTTW, Chicago's Public Television Station, "Chicago's black population stretched along 22nd to 63rd streets between State Street and Cottage Grove. But the pulsing energy of Bronzeville was located at the crowded corners of 35th and State Street and 47th Street and South Parkway Boulevard (later renamed Martin Luther King, Jr. Drive). At those intersections, people came to see and be seen, shop, conduct business, dine and dance, and experience this bustling black metropolis. The crowds reflected the diverse mix of people living in the black belt: young and old, poor and prosperous, professionals and laborers." (2011)

It was Illinois Realty's practice to buy buildings and set-up up trusts or co-ops. They bought some Black owned buildings, and sold them or rented them out, as they did White ones. The problem is because of the times and being in Chicago, people took more notice, especially of the so called "White buildings."

Another similar purchase of a "White building" was at 44th & Drexel. Notice was taken because the boundaries of the Black Belt were swelling although most Negroes were staying put. The other alarming factor was that these buildings were not only in whiter or so-called better neighborhoods, but they were large, coincidently more expensive or luxury homes or apartments. This shocked some of the public, not counting the large amounts of money being passed by those of color.

From an article by Walter White of the NAACP in *The Crisis*, October, 1919:

>Much has been written and said concerning the housing situation in Chicago and its effect on the racial situation... Although many Negroes had been living in 'white' neighborhoods, the increased exodus from the old areas created a hysterical group of persons who formed 'Property Owners Associations' for the purpose of keeping intact white neighborhoods. Prominent among these was the Kenwood-Hyde Park Property Owners' Improvement Association, as well as the Park Manor Improvement Association.
>
>Early in June the writer, while in Chicago, attended a private meeting of the first named at the Kenwood Club House, at Lake Park Avenue and 47th Street. Various plans were discussed for keeping the Negroes in 'their part of the town,' such as securing the discharge of colored persons from positions they held when they attempted to move into 'white' neighborhoods [same area & plan used against family], purchasing mortgages of Negroes buying homes and ejecting them when mortgage notes fell due and were unpaid, and many more of the same caliber...
>
>In a number of cases during the period from January 1918, to August 1919, there were bombings of colored homes and houses occupied by Negroes outside of the 'Black Belt.' During this period no less than twenty bombings took place, yet only two persons have been arrested and neither of the two has been convicted, both cases being continued. (unk.)

Even with imminent danger, inroads were made in property ownership. Each instance brought cause to be published as well as the purchase details which were common during these times. Everyone, thanks to the media, knew who you were, where you lived, and what you had done or were about to do. My great-grandfather and father wrote a prospectus for a community-owned bank and submitted it to Binga and later trustees for LaSalle National Bank. George was one of the founders of First Federal Savings and Loan Association. These "S & L's" gained their name and popularity in 1930 across the country but especially in Chicago to provide ethnic financing for homes. These were publicized with Papa's photo, office address, and home addresses.

There was that ugly rumor that some Blacks, the athlete and entertainer who were doing well, might move into a White neighborhood, which was a little more acceptable because of their celebrity status. The educated businessman, professor, realtor, attorney, or doctor they could not savor; they weren't ready to let people of color into the mainstream, and definitely not exceed their status in the middle or upper class. The outrage was that some Negroes had money!

Forgotten was the fact that regardless of income, Blacks wanted the same things as Whites, or any color, which was to provide a better future for themselves and their family. The middle and lower classes weren't trying to just move out or up and out; they just wanted to live better.

This was something else that added fuel to the fire on the concocted conspiracy theory by Camille and Cicero about my family and the Clarks. The only conspirators were the Town of Cicero, Camille De Rose, and her Cicero realtors misguided by racism and money.

There were many issues floating in the air in Chicago, but a critical one was economic class. Racism was, is about money. Cicero was a working class "sundown" city. Life was hard enough without having a middle class Negro living near you and like you.

The Chicago Council Against Racial and Religious Discrimination's statement written by Harry Jack was one of the only articles that mentioned this problem that I believe was one of the core issues as I learned from growing up in Chicago. On July 22, 1951, he wrote a statement from Rev. Hughes of the Millard Ave. Baptist Church, "'The people of Cicero did not respect the rights of their fellow Americans. . . Most of the property owners seem more concerned about the dollar and cents value of their land than they do about the rights of a fellow American. What they do not seem to realize is that when Negro families move into an area that rents almost immediately increase.'"

Yet, they fault the Black buyer not the White seller; go figure. This sets the tone for what the real estate business was like for my father and great-grandfather. Although, my great-grandfather had it easier because he would pass as white in dealings and had my great-grandmother's money to invest. My father fought the true battle because his appearance was obvious.

The *Chicago Daily Tribune* wrote on November 18, 1948, that:

'Building With Void Covenant Is Sold As Co-op For Negroes' – Purchase of the three-story 18 apartment building at the southeast corner of Drexel Blvd. and 44th St. for a reported $255,000 by a Negro syndicate, yesterday disclosed plans for converting the property into a cooperative for Negro occupancy. The buying group is headed by John W. Williams, real estate operator, and Dean Chandler and Charles Edwards, owners of Illinois Realty company, 3458 S. State St. The seller was the Liberty National Bank, trustee.

The building has had white occupancy under restrictive covenant which was voided by a Supreme Court decision, Shelley vs. Kraemer in 1948 and the precedent, Hansberry vs. Lee (1940). The apartments have five, six, seven, and nine rooms each all with two or more baths, and are being sold at $7,100, $8,520, $9,940, and $12,780. Cash down payments range from $3,000 to $5,940. The property is being financed with $110,000 mortgage." (p. 1, early ed., print)

The *Chicago Sun Times* wrote on Nov. 19, 1948:

'Negroes Fix Curbs on Apartments' –Restrictions to maintain the character of a luxurious apartment property at 44th St. and Drexel Blvd., just purchased by a Negro syndicate, were announced by Everett Levy, attorney for the purchaser.

The property includes two buildings at 4401-4409 Drexel Blvd. and 917-921 E. 44th St. It was sold by the Liberty National Bank as trustee for $225,000 to the Trust Co. of Chicago as trustee for the Cooperative Corp.

The 18 apartments, which have been occupied by white tenants, will be sold to Negro professors, doctors, and lawyers under restrictions that they may not subdivide into multiple dwelling units.

Until the U. S. Supreme Court held that restrictive covenants were not enforceable in the courts, Negroes had been barred from the buildings by covenants.

All apartments have at least two bath a piece. They will be sold for down payments of $3,300 for each of the three 5-room apartments; $3,960 for each of the nine 6-room apartments; $4,620 for each of three 7-room apartments, and $5,940 for each of the three 9-room apartments.

The buyer will also sign notes for $760 a room.

The purchasing syndicate is headed by John W. Williams, a real estate broker; Dean Chandler and Charles Edwards. The

Illinois Realty Co., 3458 S. State St., will manage the project. (p. 3, first ed.)

News of the "Goings on" spread as the syndicate, the colored syndicate, or "Negro Bloc" was on the move.

Illinois Realty's listing photo for the Walgreen Mansion (Edwards, C.)

The Pittsburgh Courier wrote on March 19, 1949:

'Pay $45,000 for Walgreen Mansion' – The Chicago and Northern District Association of Federated Women Clubs last week closed negotiations for the purchase of the imposing Walgreen mansion at 4441 S. Drexel Avenue, for the club's headquarters it was announced Saturday...

Purchase price was quoted at $45,000. Agent in the transaction was Charles Edwards of the Illinois Realty.

The structure is a three-story building with 32- by 250-foot frontage and has 32 rooms. It has been the residence of the family of Charles Walgreen, the drugstore tycoon. (unk.)

This was their business. Just as my father issued insurance claims in 1951 on May 5th under the Hartford Steam Boiler Inspection and Insurance Company and on May 25th under the London and

Lancashire Co. for Mrs. De Rose and her building. Also a letter to an insurance broker, Kralovec and Co., dated May 25th, was hand delivered on May 28th requesting new assignments.

Dad had Mrs. De Rose sign papers for workmen's comp, utilities, and insurance; rent was collected and deposited. Things were going smoothly until Mrs. De Rose finally put two and two together on her next visit to Papa's office where she met the real Mrs. Adams. At this point she found out that not only was Papa colored but that he was married. With this insult to injury, she changed her mind about her savior.

She started complaining more and more to Attorney Adams and her Cicero lawyer, and after her alarming visit she started complaining to Cicero town officials about Attorney Adams. Early on one can see that Mrs. De Rose was enamored with Papa or Attorney Adams and thought highly of him. The same was true in regards to her positive thoughts about Dad and the rest of our family. Mrs. De Rose has my father as one of the first people interested in her apartment and her furniture; which according to him was not true. He merely met her on a professional basis having bought property not too long ago near family. My parents had no inkling to buy furniture, move, and especially to rent way out in Cicero far from his business, her work, and their family. Camille made up this notion of my parents moving and buying her furniture.

Camille averred in her book, "I signed a document to the Illinois Interracial Commission stating, 'On account of the above condition, I arranged to sell my furniture and to lease my apartment to Charles Edwards who is a World War II veteran with an honorable discharge, a law student, and his wife and baby. He has been engaged in the real estate business for sometime. He and his wife are very decent, respectable persons, and well educated. They would add dignity and credit to any neighborhood in which they lived." (p. 319)

Her opinions fluctuated with her mood and disposition. This waffling was stoked by her contacts with her family and outsiders who did not understand her relationship with Adams, and the continued static she got from Cicero officials, lawmen, attorneys, and her tenants.

As we will see, when her emotions soured on my great-grandparents, father, and aunt, she turned against them both in attitude and action. Camille ranted on and on about my family; one of her differing summations as to the cause of the riot was, "The original 'dummy' to spearhead for the pretended moving into Cicero was to have been Edwards, not Harvey Clark. Clark was later decided upon because of his war record and detachment from scandal. Edwards would be less convincing especially as he was in real estate business and did have an apartment and furniture." (p. 140)

The Clarks, Harvey and Johnetta, had an apartment and furniture, too. Albeit it the landlady needed to put someone else in their apartment instigating their move. More misinformation by Ms. De Rose was that my father was to be the "dummy" for the move which had no truth. My father had no criminal record or scandals until the Cicero Riot, and served in the armed services, too. As a student he was a member of the U. S. Signal Corp Reserve from 1942 to 1943. His Armed Services Training Programs (ATSP) were: Electronics at Illinois Institute of Technology, Pre-Med at Penn State College, and Engineering at Howard University. He is a member of the famed Prometheans and at the time besides owning his own business, was in law school, was a certified real estate and insurance broker, a journeyman electrician, and married with two children.

Mrs. De Rose used Mr. Adams and Mr. Edwards as her scapegoats. She believed that they were the ones causing trouble, and the reasons why her tenants complained about the rent being raised and the need to inventory for insurance purposes. When she was called into the Cicero Rent Control Office she said that, "Negroes were taking over her building." (p. 320) Now, who started the race riot?

Ms. De Rose went on to say that, "The first complaint to the police came from a tenant's mother in law, that her daughter-in-law was very sick because Negroes [my father and great-grandmother] may come into her apartment to collect the rent. . . The lady replied that if her daughter-in-law should lose her baby that she would hold me legally responsible; that she fears the baby will be marked ... 'You can't expect to pay rent and to get a receipt from a Negro. They might touch a person's hand. Why I shudder to think of touching the hand of a Negro.'" (p. 116)

Camille talked to her lawyer in Cicero again, sought counsel from the City of Cicero's attorney, and advice from the Rent Control Board about Attorney Adams. "It should be observed that the rent office attorney had spoken to Mr. Adams many times in their office, and that the attorney did not know that Mr. Adams was the Negro lawyer that he was objecting to." (p. 126)

Camille's tirade continued because of her disappointment over her alienation of affection by my great-grandfather. It escalated even more so when the Rent Control Office produced documents that she claimed she signed but did not read, "As was her custom." Those documents mentioned Papa's wife, who Camille thought was Jewell instead of Minerva:

> When I later saw the document I noticed the name of Jewel Young. I asked who Jewel Young was. He said that Jewel Young was his wife's maiden name, and that it would be better not to let anyone know who had purchased the building. . . He said that he would move into the building. I called to his attention the objection to colored people in Cicero. He said that neither his wife nor he could be identified as colored, and called my attention to the fact that he is generally regarded as white. He also said that even if they learned that he was 'mixed' that while they might show some resentment at first that they soon would become friendly and exchange courtesies. That had happened before. He had moved into white neighborhoods and had that experience. (p. 131)

Several tenants decided to leave rather than pay the rent increase, which meant apartments were available. There was some interest in her vacated apartment and it was shown to prospective tenants by my father. My parents came out to view the apartment with my aunt, on March 25, 1951, for business reasons and curiosity.

After going out to a night club on March 31st, Camille panicked when the police and neighbors came by to see her. She called Papa, which she recounted:

> Adams advised me to stay in, not to go out until about nine in the morning when he would come out. I called him again in the morning. I told him that I was frightened, that I heard someone in the hall listening at my door. Later I called again. . . At that moment Adams and Edwards arrived in a car. The detectives got out of their cars to meet them talking to each other and waving their hands. Then Adams walked toward the building while Edwards remained outside, apparently because Edwards was identified as a Negro. I opened the door and watched Adams come up the stairs. When he entered the apartment I asked him what the detectives said. He said that no Negroes may enter the building. (p. 134)

From my father's 1951 records, he shows that he and my great-grandfather met with Berkos, Town of Cicero Attorney and Konovsky, Cicero Chief of Police, on April 1st, and that he picked up the keys to

Apt. C-5 on April 2nd from Mrs. De Rose. Camille remarks about selling her furniture to my parents, "Edwards said he would let Adams know what he would decide. Edwards made no reply regarding the furniture by March 28th. On that day Adams and I got together to pro-rate the taxes, rent, and expenses. He drew up an agreement, which both he and I signed, whereby he undertook to pay one-half of the accrued real estate taxes amounting to about $728, in payment for my furniture. He said if he would sell the furniture for more; he would give me the difference." (p. 132) So, the furniture burned was not hers as she lied about, but rather my family's.

The same records document that he later showed the place on May 19th to Dr. Geary, May 28th and 29th to S. McClure, and June 4th to Grumwell & Willis. On June 5th the Clarks viewed the same Apt. C-5 with Chandler subsequently placing a deposit on the 6th with Dad in his office. Because of their living conditions, the Clarks decided to take the place and move in as quickly as possible.

6319 W. 19th St. in April 1951 (Edwards, C.)

At the time Harvey E. Clark, Jr., 29, and his wife, Johnetta (nee Sharpe), 26, who met and married while at Fisk University needed a place to stay closer to his job for themselves and their two girls. After Mr. Harvey's tour of duty as an aviation instructor at Tuskegee he moved his family to Chicago where he got a job as a bus driver requiring him to commute twenty-five miles each way to work.

According to Mr. Harvey in his interview for the November 1951 issue of *Our World Magazine*, "'The whole mess [Cicero Riot] was started when innocently enough I tried to move my family into a Cicero apartment. I just wanted to get my wife and kids out of Chicago's filthy slums. . .I didn't know anything about Cicero, except that it was closer to my work.'" (p. 15-19)

The Clarks signed a lease and arranged to move in the first Friday of June. "On June 8th, Charles S. Edwards, the rental agent, went to the apartment with Mrs. George C. Adams. At 2:30 pm a moving van with Mr. and Mrs. Harvey E. Clark drove to the building." (1951 transcript)

The police refused to let them in, and threatened them. In an affidavit by Charles Edwards, "'About 6 pm the Chief of Police of Cicero [Konovsky] rushed out of the alley nearby followed by about twenty men and rushed up and grabbed my arm. The police in the cars out front got out of their cars and rushed up towards us. . . He hit me about eight times. . .we reached my car, I opened the door and the chief shoved me inside and pointed a revolver at my head.'" (p. 16)

My father recently repeated that that they [Cicero Police & officials] threatened his life and that the police also grabbed and shoved my great-grandmother physically moving her and pushing her into his car all the while cursing both of them, calling them foul things and of course the most common demeaning word, "Nigger." He recalls that neither the Clarks nor Scotts were beaten just pushed; it was just he who was hit repeatedly.

Dad's full affidavit to the Chicago Civil Liberties Committee reads:

> I, Charles S. Edwards, age 29 years, an American citizen of Negro ancestry, residing at 921 E. 44th Street, Chicago, Illinois, County of Cook, request the aid of the Chicago Civil Liberties Committee to uphold my constitutional rights and I make the following statement of the facts as the basis for legal action to be taken on my behalf in the federal and state courts, to vindicate my civil rights under the law.
>
> On Friday, June 8, 1951, I was the renting agent for Atty. George C. Adams, attorney for the LaSalle National Bank and Trust Co. as Trustee under Trust Agreement No. 13224, in renting of an apartment in the building 6139 W. 19th St., Cicero, Illinois. I am a licensed real estate broker. I had contracted with Mr. and Mrs. Harvey Evans Clark, Americans of Negro ancestry,

who have two children, to lease the apartment for one year at $60 per month. The apartment in question had been vacated by Mrs. Camille De Rose, who was the former owner of the entire building. The apartment is #C-5 on the second floor of the two story building.

On this day June 8, 1951, I drove out to the Apt. building and arrived about 12 noon with Mrs. George C. Adams. When we arrived there were two plain clothes policemen who met us and whom I have seen there on perhaps 10 previous occasions when I have been out to the building in the past month and a half with Atty. Adams and prospective renters. These two officers greeted us and we went up to the Apartment. We waited for the moving truck to bring the new tenants from Chicago and two squad cars came and left during about the two hours while the first two policemen remained. About 2:30 PM I saw the Maurice Scott L. S. Furniture Co. moving truck drive up in front of the entrance to the building and Mr. and Mrs. Harvey E. Clark got out of the truck and came to the building entrance to come up to their apartment. They were stopped by the two plain clothes police officers mentioned above and told they could not enter the building. I saw this and went down to the entrance and asked the policemen what was wrong and they said that the Clarks are not going to go into the building and that no furniture was going to be moved in or moved out. I asked why – and again these policemen repeated that they were going to prevent any moving in by the Clarks. These officers told us to wait there at the building entrance until the Chief of Police of Cicero, Ill. came to talk to us and one of the policemen went to telephone to the chief. I suggested to Mrs. Clark that she go with me up to the apartment and wait there with Mrs. Adams during the delay. I took her up and introduced her to Mrs. Adams and returned to the entrance to stay with Mr. Clark and the policemen waiting for the Chief of Police of Cicero.

One of the two officers said that we did not have a permit to move furniture in or out of the building. He said, 'I want all of you out of the building.' He ordered me to go upstairs and get the two women and bring them out. The policeman followed me closely and as we started up the stairs he drew out his service revolver and held it in his right hand. When we got to Apt. C-5 this policeman pointed his revolver at the two women and me and said: 'All of you get out of here right away – we are all going out.' We left the building with the officer following us with a drawn revolver in his hand. I was frightened at the danger of being shot, and the tones of the officer were those of orders and commands. When we got outside the building the Sergt. said: 'Why don't you people go home and avoid bloodshed' – directing his remarks to the five of us who were colored. I asked the janitor 'Ted' if I could use the telephone to call Atty. Adams in Chicago and I called him and advised him of what had happened to us. This was about 3:00 PM that I reported the policeman saying that a permit was needed and he said he would call the Town Clerk. Atty. Adams asked to speak to the officer in charge.

Ted asked the Serg. to talk with Atty. Adams on the phone and the Serg. said: 'I don't want to talk to him.' There were about 20 plain clothes policemen there when we came out of the building all under the direction of the Serg. who was also in plain clothes. The crowd of police all got in their cars and sat there. This was about 3:30 PM and the four of us just stood there until about 6:00 PM – Mr. Scott went over and sat on the tailgate of his truck.

Atty. Adams called twice on the telephone – first to tell me that he was informed by a bookkeeper in the Town Clerk's office that there was no such thing as a permit to move furniture required by the Town of Cicero, Illinois. During the time that we were standing there the Minister of the Lutheran church came up to express his Christian sympathy with us but added that the people in the community were afraid of their property values, and expressed hope that there could be no bloodshed. A school teacher came up and expressed his approval of our moving in. He chatted with us for some time and was the only person in the crowd of on-lookers who gathered with the coming of the police – who made us feel welcome. The crowd of on-lookers was in no way hostile or menacing by words or gestures.

About 6 PM the Chief of Police of Cicero rushed out to the alley nearby followed by about 20 men and rushed up and grabbed my arm. The police in the cars out front got out of their cars and rushed up towards us. The Chief said to me: 'You should know better – get going – get out of here fast. There will be no moving into this building – I'm not going to endanger the lives of 19 families for the likes of you.' During these statements the Chief held my left arm with his strong left hand and he kept hitting me in the back with his right fist, especially at my right shoulder and on my right side below the shoulder. He hit me about 8 times while he was pushing me ahead of him toward my car which was parked across the street. I was trying to walk but he was trying to make me move faster. When we reached the car I opened the door and the Chief shoved me inside and said: 'Get out of Cicero and don't come back in town or you'll get a bullet thru you.' There were 3-4 officers with the Chief. I opened the car door on the other side for Mrs. Adams to get in because I saw her standing outside. I started up the car and eased out thru the crowd which had gathered in the street. I saw Atty. Adams drive in behind me as I pulled away from the parking space and I stopped in the middle of the block to see what Mr. Adams was going to do. I saw Atty. Maurice Scott, Jr. pulled from Atty. Adams' car and I sat in my car very much afraid and not knowing what to do. I have not been back to Cicero since and my clients the Clarks have not been allowed to move into the apartment which is theirs.

Signed Charles S. Edwards; Signed and sworn to before me this 10th Day of June, 1951, Ira H. Latimer, NOTARY PUBLIC

The Clarks came back on July 10th, with my father and great-grandfather only to be met by a small crowd. The crowd became boisterous, rowdy, and profane. Egged on by the lack of concern by the police, the crowd moved in closer hurling insults and small items. After several minutes of jeers and comments, Dad, Papa, and the Clarks entered the building. They soon left the apartment, and the Clarks returned to the home of my parents on the South Side of Chicago. The next day it was announced that the Clarks would try a third time. "This time the word spread and almost 5,000 people were out. It started by kids throwing rocks, then fire, and screaming, 'We don't want niggers here,' and 'Throw Judge Barnes out.'" (*Sun-Times*)

The next morning the Clarks finally moved their furniture in with the help of the Scott Movers. Like my great-grandfather, father, and many other Blacks trying to live a better life, Attorney Scott and his father had another business, moving furniture. Approximately sixty Cook County Sheriffs and Cicero Police came out as requested by the moving party, but did nothing as they were attacked by rocks, bottles, etc. defying a June 24th court order by Judge Barnes to protect the "Negroes."

One newsman wrote:

U. S. District Court Judge John P. Barnes issued a restraining order against Cicero officials on June 24th. At issue was the duty of officials to protect Harvey Clark, Jr., Negro veteran of World War II, and his family.

Barnes' order named the town president, police chief, clerk, and trustees. It alleged that police had mistreated Clark and others helping him to move into an apartment at 6139 W. 19th, in Cicero, on June 8th.

The officials and 300 Cicero residents were in Judge Barnes court when he issued the order.

'Transcript Quoted' – According to the transcript Town Attorney Nicholas Berkos contended that the Cicero police were trying to 'protect 19 families and all of the children' in the apartment building.

Judge Barnes replied, 'I'll tell you what you have to do. You will have to exercise the same diligence to see that these folks who are called Negroes get into that apartment and stay there peacefully as you have been exercising to keep them out.

I don't care what the past history of that building is. That is of no concern to this court. You just see that that they are not interfered with or you will be in serious trouble.'

'Owner Sought' – Berkos replied he was trying to find out who is the true owner of the building, which was then in the name of Jewel Young, a niece of Atty. George C. Adams, who had designated Charles Edwards, 3456 State, as rental agent. Clark had rented the apartment from Edwards.

'Listen, you don't need to worry about who is the owner,' interrupted Judge Barnes. Unless some landlord shows you some right, you don't need to worry about that. (Sonderby, p. 1)

It is believed that the whole point of Berkos bringing up the issue of ownership was to incite the three hundred inside the court room and echo the ever-nourishing Godzilla terror in the community that not only were Negroes moving in by renting, but the most awful reality; Coloreds actually owned the building. They owned property in Cicero!

"When later I appeared before the Grand Jury which investigated before the riots, I heard the clerk call out the name of Jewel Young. An infirmed childlike underdeveloped young lady arose in response to that name. Mrs. Adams adjusted the girl's hair. Apparently Jewel Yong was brought in response to a subpoena when her name was found in the record as the person to whom the property was assigned. A feeling of pity gripped the jurors and she was asked but a few questions. This Jewel Young is not Adam's wife, of course, but as I was later informed, is a step daughter of a previous marriage." (p. 236)

After the second attempt to move in, the National Guard was requested. Gov. Stevenson ordered the men in, but they didn't start arriving until 1030 pm when the police line was broken. The Cicero Police and Cook County Sheriffs stood and watched as people entered the building throwing out furniture and then setting it on fire. (Edwards) "By 930 pm the eight police deputies and six sheriffs' men had arrested no one while the building burned down. By the end at 230 am, 19 were injured and 70 arrested." (De Rose, p. 187)

This was the first time that a major riot was filmed on television and their footage as well as photographs helped with indictments. NBC and WGN TV stations were on site, and unfortunately one of WGN's crewmembers was injured.

James Loewen in his book, *Sundown Towns*, states that Cicero is a "sundown town," and cites Arnold Hirsch about the coverage of the Cicero Race Riot, "Major white riots in Chicago after World War II got very little coverage in that city's newspapers, partly at the behest of the Chicago Commission on Human Relations. . . The riot in suburban Cicero, July 10 - 12, 1951, did get covered but not for the first two days. Only after the National Guard was called out on July 12 and after the story made the local TV news did the *Tribune* and *Sun-Times* publish anything about the now infamous act." (p. 203)

Crowds re-assembled on the 13th but there were only minor happenings. The National Guard stayed on watch for several days later until re-called.

Chapter Eight
"Can't Do Anything Right"

This chapter focuses on my father, Charles S. Edwards. The following consists of audiotapes transcribed from my father's recorder and from a CD from Georgia Public Radio's StoryCorps from February 25, 2011, and video tapes of interviews made at home.

"History is the memory of the human race; for an individual to wake up some morning with no memory would be devastating. In addition to the emotional trauma of suddenly finding everyone and everything unknown and unfathomable there would be no way to carry out the practical necessities of work or managing a home much less maintaining or establishing relationships with other human beings. We are confronted with a thriving present and a sustainable future. " (Edwards, 2006)

"Dean Chandler absconded with all of my money and Illinois Realty's from our partnership. He even took the collected rent and spent it. He disappeared and I did not know where he went. That was the disadvantage of a partnership. " (Edwards, 2009)

"Two of the outstanding accounts were the Brinkerhoff's and Redel's. Chandler was just a thief. " (Edwards, 2009)

After the riot, my wife and I took the Clark family (4 people) into our home. We did not contribute any money other than food because we had none to give or loan them at the time. We were broke. The wife and I did work out an agreement with Clara Brinkerhoff to repay the money Dean stole from her by not depositing her rent.

We also were sued by the Redels because Chandler did not deposit her rent, and they took possession of the office and all of the proceeds from office furniture and equipment.

We had to move from 921 E. 44th St. for two reasons. One was because of all of threats, the many, unending threats. We received many threats at home during the Cicero incident and many years afterwards. The second reason was when our home was lost.

When we purchased the building at 44th and Drexel with the investor Williams, we converted it into a co-op with great difficulties from a professor from the University of Chicago. Our mortgage and the entire building were foreclosed on by A. J. Sirroni in 1953.

Illinois Realty, my company, went under while I was tied up with the Cicero Indictment. Dean Chandler cleared out all of the cash that he could get his hands on. (Edwards, 2009)

Our company, Illinois Realty, formed in 1948, after I got my real estate broker's and insurance broker's licenses, was not incorporated. We had an office in the Binga or Arcade Building at 3458 S. State, Suite 415. Mr. Adams defended Jesse Binga, former African-American Pullman porter in a law suit in regards to his opening and closing the first Negro owned bank in Chicago. Later the building was taken over by the Illinois Institute of Technology. Illinois Realty specialized in mortgages, sales, insurance, and management of property. (Edwards, 2011)

My great-grandparents had more of an advantage than my father and his company in buying large previously white-owned and occupied properties before the Shelly v. Kraemer decision in 1948; my great-grandfather went alone to close and my father paid his law professor and associate to represent him. Sometimes Dad's practice backfired because Attorney Edward Lewy was Jewish. Other large properties sold by Illinois Realty included a sixteen room home in the block of 4800 and Ellis to Rev. Muhammad, and the Walgreens Building at 4441 S. Drexel Boulevard with thirty-two rooms to an organization.

Negro Co-ops on the Southside of Chicago were booming as restrictive covenants fell. Besides 921 E. 44th St., there was the 122 apartment, 21-story building at 5530 Lake Shore Dr., the one at 63rd and South Park with over 600 units, and the twin 25 story towers on South Shore Dr. by other syndicates.

"What prompted us to do a cooperative came in the sense of empowerment of us and others. This was a good way to make a profit prior to condominiums, and an easier alternative to buying a single family home for most when space and money were issues after the depression and during and after the war. The problems weren't in the business of running the co-op but in the area, the times, and that the building was formerly all-white." (Edwards, 2011)

S. I. Hayakawa in his column, "Second Thoughts," for The *Chicago Defender* on June 23, 1945, wrote about the, "'Difficulties of Negro Co-ops' – Having strongly urged the formation of consumer co-operatives among Negroes, I should say something about the special difficulties confronting Negro co-operatives. Of Course, there is no such thing as Negroes, 'as a race,' being any less (or more) able to run co-operatives than other people. Nevertheless, it cannot be denied that the common experience of American Negroes in a world largely hostile to them has left many of them hurt and handicapped." (p. 13)

Dad comments, "We had no plans to buy any other buildings at the time because of the nature of the times and many incidents. The Clarks were to move in because they needed a place to stay. We did not conspire to incite the riots in Cicero." (Videotape, 2011)

"Never saw the Clarks or Camille De Rose in later years after the Cicero Riot lawsuits were settled [post 1957]. I don't recall the disposition of the NAACP's $200,000 Civil Law Suit using my name; if there was any money Mr. Adams probably got it." (Interview, 2011)

"Mr. Adams' involvement with the Scott's [Clarks' movers] started when he represented Maurice, Jr. for his Section 8 hearing when he was being dishonorably discharged from the military. He wanted to go to law school and Papa got the matter cleared up. Papa also represented the father, Maurice, Sr., who was indicted for keeping a white woman captive in his apartment. It was proven that the relationship was consensual." (Edwards, 2009) [Other relatives commented that Papa won the case by proving she was on her period by producing feminine products, and he was impotent.]

"In the John Marshall Law School final comprehensive exams, I fell asleep in the classroom. I had worked all night and I went to class; I didn't even start any of the exams." (Edwards, 2011)

"It was the nature of the times. I was involved in other incidents, like forming a union and leading the strike with local 204 on April 15, 1941, where I was the Chief Steward and President of the Union during the strike." (Edwards, 2010)

"I started at Greiss-Pfleger Tanning Company on September 28, 1940, as a sorter's helper handling the hides. I joined the union in January 1941 and was one of about 206 Negroes, who were all employed in the sorting and cleaning of hides in the 'Wet' department, a real nasty, dirty physical job. There were 536 citizens and 63 aliens and 25 nationalities, with 590 in the union out of 599. All skilled jobs were held by European born workers. The Jewish foreman from the maintenance department took notice of how hard I worked and expressed his desire to diversify his department, so I became an electrician in training." (Edwards, Autobiography, 1970)

"The strike was settled on May 23rd where we got $250,000 in raises, 2 to 3 cents extra for handling large hides, new rates, re-vamped swing shifts, 10 minute morning and lunch period breaks, improvement of work facilities, and re-instatement of discharged employees." (Edwards' Strike Notes, 1941)

On September 5, 1942, my father wrote the following letter to Local 204 International Fur and Leather Workers Union:

> It has become necessary that I relinquish the position of trust which you have placed in me. I regretfully leave the office of Chief Steward after holding it but a brief while. I have endeavored by the earnest work I have put into the Local since its origin to give service to a cause I am strongly moved by. I trust that you feel that I have had some measure of success.
>
> My departure for the Signal Corps School was unavoidably sudden. Along with a number of others, I am now receiving training in electronics under the supervision and control of the war department. At the completion of our training, we go into active service with training that will better enable us to render assistance in defeat of the Axis and Nipponese lords.
>
> It is with all sincerity that I admonish you to strengthen your war efforts, to redouble your support of the allied cause, and to build your local. Each is important. The nation's democratic form of existence is threatened. American labor is in peril of its birthright of a free country. Each of us must do and sacrifice for his bit toward bringing this conflict to an early victory.
>
> I expect to hear of great things from Local 204. There are darker, more fruitless periods ahead, but we must foresee the value the Local will be in unitedly helping to 'win the war,' in solidly preserving the progress of labor, and in successfully aiding toward stabilizing the economic condition which inevitably is induced by wars.

I hope to hear from as many of my friends who will take time to write me.

Fraternally and sincerely yours,
Charles S. Edwards, Jr. (Edwards, 1942)

Another incident was when I enlisted and was sent out to Camp McDowell where I was trained in radar and radar maintenance. When I went into the service I went to Ft. Custer first where I sat in a barrack for a week because my records showed my race as 'White.' Eventually, they manipulated my records resulting in my finally being able to put on the uniform. I was shipped off to Salt Lake City. Unfortunately when I got there I tried o go to the PX, they said no. Then the next day I tried to go to the Chapel, and they said no. The next thing I went into the theatre and had just gotten myself comfortable when they turned the lights on. An announcement came saying that they had a reserve section for certain troops, and one person was not seated in the reserved section. I did not move and the next thing the MP's came and escorted me out of the theatre. When I got outside I started my tirade about all of the bad things that happened to me at the camp, so I was thrown in the brigade.

I stayed there until a group from Washington, D. C. came to interview me for Officers Candidate School to become a Second Lieutenant. I was accepted into the Quartermaster's Corp in summer of 1945 and sent to Ft. Barkeley, Texas. We were trying to catch a bus and several passed us by, when finally I decided to commandeer one of the buses. The driver called his boss who said to change the sign from 'White Only' to 'Colored.' Finally we were able to go into town.

Afterwards I found myself back at Camp Crowder in medical training; twice I was sent to pick up prisoners. One was White that we brought all the way back from Pennsylvania. Traveling was difficult because we could not sit in either designated [race] area so we ended up in storage or livestock box cars.

I requested a discharge on June 22, 1945, because both parents were very ill. (Edwards, 2010)

His letter to the Commanding General of the same date read:

> My father is totally disabled and recently has been committed to a convalescent home. He is not receiving the attention that his condition warrants. My presence will mean that he can return home. My mother is seriously ill with an incurable heart condition which prevents her from living at home. This condition has arisen since my entrance into the

army. Hospital bills are accumulating and greatly worry my parents and myself...I feel that I am desperately needed at home to provide a home for my parents and to tend to their urgent needs. (Edwards, 1945)

Both his parents and the couple he thought were his grandparents died within a year and a half of his release.

"After my honorable discharge, I returned to Greiss Tanning Company then enrolled in Roosevelt College and stayed at 5350 S. Michigan where I became a Republican Captain of the 37th Precinct, 3rd Ward, with Bill King as Committeeman. " (Edwards, 1945)

"On the day of the riot, I received a note from Chandler. It read, 'IMP –CSE, 7/10/51 @ 2:45 pm - Clark will call Scott's furniture store about 5 pm. VI 2-0723. He has been advised by Adams to have armed guard for night. Adams was supposed to get colored deputy but if he can't, Clark wants to know if you will go. (Adams said you would.) Call and leave word with Scott Jr.'s wife and where he will meet you. He is taking kids to Gary and is to meet armed escort (Sheriff) at 26th & California at 8 pm.' " (Edwards reading note from 1951)

When things died down after the riot and recovering from Dad's partner's theft, my mother returned to modeling which she did earlier from March 1, 1947, on to help out with the bills. She had done runway work previously but now was doing photo work and making appearances at social events, like galas for the Provident Hospital, Bud Biliken, etc. She also became an instructor for a modeling school and a lead model for the Designer School of Dressmaking.

Money was quite difficult. My parents borrowed from family members and stayed with them for months, moving from one family household to another. One note by my father on the back of a card stuck in the middle of the riot's legal docs read, "Life is but a moment lost in the whirling abyss of eternity, prolonged exasperation." (Edwards, 1952)

With my great-grandmother's activity of going to the racetrack daily and my mother having gone with her and having had previous luck, she started taking the little money they had to bet on horses. As is with most cases, she was lucky when she didn't need the money, but very unlucky when she did, losing $400 for one season. Their debts grew and caused a rift in their marriage with thoughts even of divorce; she wrote him a long letter.

His response was a poem in all capitals to her when she was trying to decide what to do that read:

'WHAT CAN I DO' –
HOW DID IT HAPPEN?
I CAN'T EXPLAIN;
IT'S JUST ONE OF THOSE THINGS,
THAT HAD TO BE.
WHAT CAN I DO,
TO MEND YOUR HEART,
TO MAKE AMENDS,
FOR ALL THE THINGS, I DIDN'T MEAN TO DO.
MY ONE DESIRE;
WAS TO BE A HELP,
BUT THE TABLES WERE TURNED,
AND NOW – THE DAMAGE IS DONE.
WHAT CAN I DO,
TO MAKE AMENDS,
FOR ALL THE THINGS,
THAT MAKE YOU BLUE. (Edwards, 1952)

Obviously, sixty-three years later, they worked through this. In the meantime, my mother in between modeling assignments went back to work for Humiston-Keeling at 3900 S. State taking pharmaceutical orders. Later in 1954, they recovered and bought their first single family home at 5950 S. Loomis. Mom was a housewife from April 15, 1954 to 1959, after giving birth to four more kids in 1954, 1955, 1957, and 1958. Then she taught Kindergarten to third grade at Catholic and public schools; taking off in 1965 to give birth to her seventh and eighth children, although, one of the twins only made it a few days.

Chapter Nine
"They Did It; I Saw Them"

Camille De Rose asserted that, "This lawyer [George Adams] deliberately organized the race riots which destroyed my home. I did not know that he was not a white man. I did not know that he was 'mixed,' yet even if I knew I would not have known that he would bring the riots to my home." (p. 290)

Mrs. De Rose's opinion of my great-grandfather changed as the wind does in Chicago. Here are some examples taken in order from her book. "I fled for my life into the shelter of an elderly Attorney At Law, a man of learning, a member of a profession bound by its ethics." (p. 138) "Adams continued to show a fatherly interest in me." (p. 140) "Yes, as I said, I staunchly relied upon my redeemer, my attorney. After the storms of the riots died down, I found myself again in Adams' office." (p. 160) "That Adams is a scalawag and that the organization [NAACP] itself was not what it should be." (p. 246) "The first blow came from: George C. Adams: lawyer, publisher and author, statesman, real estate and loans, rental agency, banker, radio commentator, orator, spiritualist and minister, real estate owner, insurance agent, oil stock broker, Detective Agency." (p. 335)

De Rose alleges that, "There was no intention of having Harvey E. Clark, or any Negro, move into my building." (p. 12) Accordingly, charges were brought against my father and great-grandfather. She became so mad at my great-grandfather that she became one of the key witnesses for the City of Cicero and Cook County. However, this all backfired. October 1952, Papa successfully defended himself against criminal fraud against Camille. He later filed a damage suit for $400,000 against Camille, her friend Francis Walker, and Attorneys Cook, Payne, and Carter.

Talk about persona non grata; that would be my summation of Camille De Rose. She spoke often and frequently about being color blind but almost every reference is to color, liken to Metro Chicago's color panic in 1951. The riot was on account of the quest of the Clark family to move into an apartment in Cicero. It wasn't until the Civil Rights Acts of 1968 that banned discrimination in the sale or rental of housing. Still some people discriminated and certain areas did not integrate or became "sundown," like small towns and areas in Metro Chicago.

NAACP's Attorneys Thurgood Marshall and George Leighton, Realtor Charles Edwards, Attorney George Adams, Attorney Joe Clayton, Attorney Maurice Scott, and Harvey and Johnetta Clark meet Cicero Officials. (Adams, M.)

Mrs. De Rose continued her chant of conspiracy, "We can point to the so-called 'Cicero Race Riots.' Those riots were deliberately planned by Attorney Adams and followed through by the NAACP. Negroes and Orientals are not new to Cicero. Had Harvey Clark truly intended to live in my building, he might have moved into it quietly, as I said before... But such was not the intention at all. The NAACP membership had been dwindling and their leaders were hard put for an occasion to support a drive for funds and memberships. At the same time Attorney Adams found a situation which he could maneuver to support claims and lawsuits. He therefore staged a Roman holiday for entry of the Clarks and Adams to take over in Cicero." (p. 319)

"Therefore the scheme of 'moving' the Clark's to Cicero was to keep the Clark's and others on the South Side. It did more! It whipped up excitement about 'civil rights,' discrimination, and race hatred. . . The plan worked so good for the NAACP that other rival groups rushed in to get some of the flood of gold. It also gave support for a lawsuit against the town of Cicero for $200,000. In other words the riots paid off." (p. 322)

Camille was wrong, quite wrong. There were plans to move in to 6319 S. 19th St. on several peoples' parts, and there was no conspiracy to riot as was proven in court after charges were filed against my family and the Clarks, and the judge ruled on their behalf. There was no clandestine plan to cause attention or burn a building to bring attention to anyone or anything. Who would want to purposely ruin their life and that of their loved ones? The reason the police, etc. were notified was for protection on the second attempt. Why would anyone think that they wouldn't be protected? On the third time they got legal assistance; again this did not matter. Those of color, the colored workers Camille saw, left at sunset, unless they were quarantined in the cinder block area of the racetrack all night.

It was the "Ciceronian's," the white citizens of Cicero that caused the damage and started the violence. They were aided and abetted by the Cicero town officials, the Cicero Police, the Cook County's Sheriff Department, and Camille. What was not understood at that time, or didn't want to be tolerated is that Blacks just wanted a better life for themselves and their families. Furthermore, walking into your own property is not a crime; neither is renting it out, or leasing an apartment.

Fifty-five years later, Cicero still seems to shirk responsibility, only to plant the seed of innuendo by blaming realtors on their town website:

> 'Cicero vs. civil rights' - Yet Cicero's reputation would sink even lower during the Civil Rights period. Ever wary of outsiders, Cicero was protective of what it had. Residents

realized their neighborhoods were ripe for the type of block-by-block 'white flight' (often orchestrated by unscrupulous Realtors) that was occurring in the nearby West Side neighborhoods of Chicago to the north. The concept of a diverse or 'mixed' community was alien at the time. Racial tensions continued to mount as residents resisted African Americans moving in. Cicero was considered a 'sundown town,' which meant blacks could shop or work there during the day but were unwelcome after nightfall.

In July 1951, during the same year Dr. Percy Julian's home was firebombed when he moved into Oak Park, a 'race riot' occurred in Cicero. When black CTA bus driver and World War II veteran Harvey Clark, Jr. and his family attempted to move into an apartment at 6139 19th Street, just seven blocks south of Oak Park, they were met by an angry mob that destroyed their belongings, trashed the building, and rioted for the next three days and nights. At its peak, the out-of-control disturbance involved as many as 5,000 white protesters who fought police and deputies. Gov. Adlai Stevenson had to activate five companies of National Guardsmen to restore order. This 'race riot' drew worldwide condemnation. At a subsequent court hearing, many people wore large medallions bearing the inscription, 'Keep Cicero White.' No one was ever punished.

When Rev. Martin Luther King Jr. threatened to march through Cicero because of the town's history of intolerance, he was advised such a protest would be a 'suicide mission.' Over 250 demonstrators did 'march on Cicero' on Sunday, Sept. 4, 1966 - without Dr. King, however. Over 3,000 police and National Guardsmen were on hand to 'protect' the town. Though 38 hecklers (no marchers) were arrested for disorderly conduct and resisting arrest, the predicted 'explosion of violence' never occurred. Thus, during the turbulent '60s, Cicero's reputation as a gangland hideout was surpassed by its resistance to integration. The town was now perceived as anti-black as well as anti-law.

Many people still remember that period very well. Some folks loaned photos they'd taken with their own cameras, showing the marching National Guard troops and the jeering crowds packed along the sidewalks. No one I spoke to was proud of that era or glad about how their community responded.

They simply described that day as a dark piece of local history, as unavoidable as a tornado. (Deucher, 2006)

Papa several times talked about tolerance to us, especially when telling stories. His father Charles, "C. J.", or "Pa" was White and his mother, "Ma," Violet was a Mulatto. (We are not sure whether she was White and Black, White and Native American, or all three.) In Chicago they lived at 23 E. 36th Pl. which was near the color line. Family members remember Ma being blind in her later years, possibly from glaucoma or cataracts.

I find a George Adams in the Dawes Territorial Records as a Choctaw Freedman in approximately 1902 at 24, which is the right age, along with a Choctaw freedman by the name of Vina (records?) Gibson. (This is the listed maiden name of his mother on documents that he wrote.) at age 39. However, the Gibson surname could just be an acquired name picked from nearby Ft. Gibson or the family did not voluntarily register with the Dawes Rolls.

This last theory fits the dates and ages that I have and coincides with most of the story I was told when younger and puts George in Louisiana at 15 from census. The people that he was a servant for came from Virginia which is also the birthplace that Papa puts as his father's birth state (although Mississippi and Louisiana also appear), even though I have seen no proof which could add fuel to the story of his being President Adam's grandson or great-grandson, or playing on the White House lawn.

I would surmise that his mother, who on some of his documents is Violet, some it's Viola, some V, and some unknown, was forced to go to Oklahoma from Louisiana with the other four great Native American tribes as a member of the Choctaw Tribe in 1903. The 1900 Census shows the Adams Family in Rayville, LA and the 1910 Census shows the same family in Muskogee, OK. In Muskogee, they were very near to Sarah Rector, noted for being the country's richest black girl with millions from her oil well. The mystery of their move will remain unsolved.

My great-grandparents owned and lived in one to three several large properties at a time with other members of the family and family friends. Some even appeared as adopted children on the census, like Charles Rose. The large properties that they owned and lived in were:

    5742 S. Monroe Ave. (1902 –On Sam Young's Death Record);

5618 S. Harper (1915 – On Susan Campbell's Death Record);
4410 S. Vincennes – Owned & Free[no mortgage] (1920 Census, Sheet #5);
4121 South Park;
4510 S. Forestville (Earliest Mom remembers – (1925);
404 E. 48th Street;
4523 S. Calumet (1927 Article);
5700 S. Michigan (1930 Census & news articles);
5726 S. Indiana (1932 to 1942);
4439 S. Michigan (1941 to 1957);
4757 -59 South Parkway (1938 to 1954);
5138 S. Kenwood Ave. (1953 to 1998).

The property at the time of the Cicero Riot was 4757– 4759 South Parkway, originally Grand Boulevard, and in present day King Boulevard. The 30 room house was built by Geo. P. Lerthal and deeded first on October 15, 1894, to him as builder. (Chicago Plats & Tracts, 2011)

Dr. Ephraim Ingals, of Rush College, bought the place on January 7, 1895. (Chicago Plats & Tracts, 2011) "Dr. Ingals was active in the affairs of the Chicago Medical Society, serving four terms as its president from 1876-77, 1877-78, 1878-79 and from 1881 till 1882. He was also one of the presidents of the Illinois State Medical Society. In 1851 he married Miss Melissa Church and of this union were born four daughters, one of whom [Lucy] became the wife of Dr. E. Fletcher Ingals, [a nephew and doctor of laryngology]. Dr. Ephraim Ingals died December 1900 in his home [4757 Grand Boulevard.]" (Chicago Medical Society Journal, 1938)

The home stayed in the Ingals family transferring back and forth for twelve times until it was picked up by the State of Illinois on January 15, 1921. The Blackstone Institute, the first correspondence law school had it for one year, and Golfer's Magazine had it for another year. Then, George C. Adams picked up the building on May 20, 1938, by affidavit with his step-son, Siegel Young, Sr., and the whole family stayed there until 1952. They moved into another building they had bought earlier to escape the hoopla of the riot aftermath.

Chicago Land Tracts described the building as, "A huge Victorian mansion fronting a wide boulevard, Grand, and 48th Street," (Book 347, 2011) in the hub of Bronzeville, on the same block of

South Parkway as the Regal Theatre at 4719 and the Savoy Ballroom at 4701. The two entertainment buildings were part of the same campus as the South Department Store, all built and owned by the Englesteins, which opened in 1928 on 421 E. 47th St. The home at 4757 had three large white columns which ushered you onto the large veranda. Their neighbors on the same street included Robert S. Abbott, owner of the *Chicago Defender*, at 4742, and Attorney Nathan K. McGill and Family at 4806.

Unlike many of their neighbors, they had non-family members as well, on their lower floor of three. They were the poorest of the rich but fit in with the color of the so called town, "Bronzeville" of the "Black Belt" which was named aptly for some of the constituents who were of mixed ancestry. Some of their other friends, neighbors, and associates were Jesse Binga, Rev. Edward Cole (Nat King Cole's father), Joe Louis Barrow (world heavyweight boxing champ, 1937 - 1949), Dr. Clifford Doyle (Chairman of Provident Hospital General Medicine), Al Benson ("Godfather of Black Radio"), Congressman Oscar De Priest (1st of 20th century), and some of Negro Baseball's American Giant players.

A historical website of Chicago describes Bronzeville:

> The area is bounded by 39th and 51st Streets to the north and south, and by Cottage Grove Avenue and the Chicago, Rock Island & Pacific Railroad tracks to the east and west. Until 1874 when the South Parks Commission lined with trees a thoroughfare they called Grand Boulevard (Now Dr. Martin Luther King Jr. Drive), the area was a combination of prairie and thick woods. The development of this street, situated at the center of the community, made it a popular carriage route on which many of Chicago's wealthy built elegant mansions. The population of the Grand Boulevard community grew steadily throughout the latter part of the nineteenth century, attracting not only the wealthy, but middle- and working-class American-born whites of Irish, Scottish, and English origin, German, Jews, and a few African Americans.
>
> Grand Boulevard became the hub of 'Bronzeville,' the name the Chicago Bee gave to Chicago's South Side African American community. A thriving center of successful black businesses, civic organizations, and churches, Bronzeville is in every way 'a city within a city.' The large number of black intellectuals, politicians, sports figures, artists, and writers who

made their homes in Bronzeville made it a cultural mecca, the central institution of which was the famed Regal Theater located at 47th and Grand Boulevard. (http://www.encyclopedia.chicagohistory.org, 2011)

The idea of property seemed to be ingrained in my great-grandmother more then my great-grandfather as conveyed by sentiment and growing up with them. She financed George in purchasing property and her son Siegel, Sr. in a scavenger business. The business was doing quite well until 1929 when everything went belly-up; which sent Siegel, Sr. to the U. S. Government to work as a postal carrier. Minerva managed to hold onto money because of having property, and Papa's work was booming because of friends. Minerva travelled everywhere with her white poodle chauffeured by her two drivers, Sugar and Reginald Cage, in an extended black Cadillac.

Attorney Adam's income from his law firm on the 1930 Census was listed as "$36, 000," (Sheet #6A) not including Minerva's income from investment property or other ventures. The $36,000.00 in today's times [2010] would be half a million converted on Measuring Worth's Website. However, his worth comes to "$3,070,000 using the Nominal Gross Domestic Product (GDP) per capita. . . you want to know how that person ranked in status compared to what others earned so it would be best to use GDP per capita. Finally, your question may be how economically 'powerful' that person would be, and then you should use share of GDP, which would be $7,720,000 using the relative share of GDP [which divides the country's GDP by the total number of people in the country]. In 1931, an accountant in the US would be earning about $2,250, an amount that would represent a comparative purchasing power of $31,700 in current dollars. However, this salary is almost 45% more than what the average household spent in those days. This would correspond to $168,000 today, a 'status' of nearly twice the national average." (http://www.measuringworth.com/uscompare, 2010)

With Papa's help the family re-financed, made trusts, re-drew trusts, and took out new loans and mortgages. With all of these large or multi-family properties, Minerva Adams, a. k. a. Mother Adams, was able to house transient family and friends. Known as the "Harriet Tubman of Chicago," she not only brought every family member up from Louisiana, Kentucky, Tennessee, and Mississippi, but most family friends, too. I could see why she saw her "Old buddy" Casey Jones of Jackson, TN, near her hometown of Clarksville, often since the Illinois

Central Railroad's "Cannonball Express" went from Canton, MS (home of the other side of the family) to Chicago.

Mother Adams used to say at various times, "Owning property means you're not property;" and "Always keep some money for yourself." "When you go out, go with clean underwear and some money tucked away, just in case." My great-grandmother always made us save. Every allowance came in two parts; one to spend and the other went in our money saver. I still have some of my LaSalle Bank and First Federal money-savers. Sadly I spent the most valuable coin, a 1943 copper penny, for candy not knowing. I thought the silver penny was rarer, only to find out as an adult that because of the war all of the pennies that year were silver, except the first few that were pressed by mistake.

Papa would quiz us on business and news items and we were required to read one of the books from his extensive library off their bedroom. Being a child was not an option unless one of my aunts came to rescue you. Some of my fondest memories were going to Riverview with one, going to Flo's Restaurant with another, and going to the drive-in theater with another.

Other properties as the one where the Cicero Riot occurred (6319 W. 19th Street) and those held by the family in the Wood Building Corporation were just investments. I did not find any record of George owning Fannie Walker's property at 2057-59 Washington Boulevard as Camille claimed in court.

My great-grandfather tried to protect my father and the rest of the family as best he could early on during 1951 and 1952 through his detective agency, friends, family, and people he helped out in court. Notice in the following interview given by Papa that the Clarks were staying with my parents but he did not mention their name, only their address. This decision was probably encouraged by my mother and great-grandmother.

The interview for the *Chicago Tribune* on July 13, 1951, consisted of, "'Clark is a member of the American Legion,' his attorney, George C. Adams, 4757 South Parkway said. . . Adams said that, 'The Clarks now have no home, having given up their St. Lawrence Av. Apartment. They found lodgings Tuesday night in a one room apartment at 921 E. 44th St.'" Another instance of George being coy about using Charles' name was reported in the *Chicago Tribune* on March 11, 1952, "George C. Adams, Negro Attorney, with offices at 54 [wrong address-64] W. Randolph St. told a jury in Criminal Court yesterday that a Cicero policeman told him and a Negro companion, 'Get out of town and don't come back or you'll be drilled full of holes'. . .The Clarks, Adams, and a Negro companion visited the building July 8, Adams said. He said, the 'Police roughed them up,' threatened him and his companion and searched his companion for a gun." (p. 8)

While growing up Papa never said any words of endearment, nevertheless, we knew he loved us like we were his own. We met his side of the family only during funerals. Everything he did was about preparing us to live in an America that was not color blind.

The side of my great-grandfather that I never knew earlier, and have only since found out by reading old family papers, news clippings, and research in archives, was in several parts. His early days in Louisiana can only be traced by word of mouth; although, I found a 1900 Census record showing the Adams family (Charles, Violet, Frank, George, Daisy, Oscar) in Rayville, LA in Richland Parrish in northeastern Louisiana stating that Charles and Violet had been married for eighteen years. This would hold water to the theory that Violet came up to Oklahoma with the Choctaw's second migration to Oklahoma in 1903. Frank, George's oldest brother, died in 1906; I still have not found out why even though Papa mentions Frank in news articles and during church services.

I did find the Adams family (Charles, Violet, George, Daisy, Oscar, and Joshua) in Muskogee, OK in the 1910 Census, all listed as Mulatto. However, family members agree that Charles was White. I was not able to find his death certificate. Violet's death record lists no mother and only her father from Virginia by the name of George Stious. I could find nothing in the census records for this name.

The next surfacing of Papa comes in a 1914 Yearbook of the Muskogee Manual Training High School graduating class. At that time from everything I have, he would be a 25 or 30 year old senior. The history of this high school which was started in 1907 was a segregated school for Negroes in Indian Territory around the time when Oklahoma became a state. There were very few who came to Oklahoma on their own, most came as slaves from reading some of the "Afro-American - Native American," Oklahoman, and Muskogee documents, websites, and blogs.

The City of Muskogee's website gives the history of the town:
> Known as the Three Forks region, this area was the hub for the settlement and development of what became Indian Territory. One of the first and most important western military

outposts was established at Fort Gibson. Here the Five Civilized Tribes arrived after their long trek from the southeast in one of America's most poignant dramas known as the 'Trail of Tears'. . .

When the Missouri-Kansas & Texas Railroad became the first rail line to cross Indian Territory in 1872, Muskogee was born. Named for the Creek Tribe, this dusty, raucous cow town rapidly grew into Indian Territory's most important city when the U.S. government established the Union Agency for the Five Civilized Tribes in 1875. The government established a federal court here in 1889. The Dawes Commission to the Five Civilized Tribes was headquartered here to enroll the Indians and allot their land. It was in Muskogee that the Tribes gathered in 1905 to write a constitution for the State of Sequoyah. Muskogee was selected to be the capital of the 'Indian State.' Denied admission to the Union, Indian Territory then joined with Oklahoma Territory to form the great state of Oklahoma.

Manual Training High School educated 138 students in grades nine through twelve during 1916. Two-thirds were girls. Furthermore, its classrooms taught another 285 pupils in one class of the sixth grade and all of the seventh and eight grades. (http://www.muskogeehistorian.com, 2011)

At the time of this publishing, I have found many birthdates on documents, census records, and in newspapers with ages that don't jibe for George C. Adams. The main two dates have the same month and day but one is in 1884 (There were many newspaper articles with this date, even one had him in a photo celebrating his 80th birthday.) In legal articles or journals, e. g. National Bar Assoc., he has 1889. My guess is February 3, 1889, because it fits most of the more official documents that I have on him. There has been no easy course, and I must admit many an hour going off in different directions from one archive to the next upon a new clue.

I could not get any information from the Howard University Law School, or the National Bar Association which he co-founded. However, some of the National Bar Association's Journals were available in the Chicago Law Library. Papa is mentioned in the Who's Who in Colored America - (Vol. 3, Journal, 6th ed.), and in subsequent years of 1941, 1944, and 1950.

After graduation, Papa served as a clerk with the U. S. Army in Washington, D. C. before starting his practice. Later, he moved to Chicago, where he passed the bar in Illinois, Wisconsin, Iowa, and

Oklahoma, and started practicing in Chicago in 1919. He is first documented there in the 1920 census as a "Lodger." He married my great-grandmother on December 7, 1921, and in the 1930 census you see them together in their first home.

In the twenties, Papa established himself as an orator and had an unique ability to get significant cases. However, to my understanding, he kept his public world different from his private world as he was passing when convenient as his first Chicago address, 2030 Maypole, was in an all white area. His second address, 515 Grand Blvd., was in a fringe area; his block had 13 Mulatto, 8 Black, & 6 White members which was highly unusual for Chicago in 1919/1920.

The Adams' address in 1923 was 4410 S. Vincennes which was just across the border; here is where he met my great-grandmother looking for a place to rent. At that time the "Black Belt," or black boundaries, were 26th Street to the north, 55th Street to the south, State Street to the west, and Lake Michigan to the east.

Cohen and Taylor in their book, *American Pharaoh: Mayor Richard J. Daley*, wrote:

> The Black Belt provided Chicago's blacks with a measure of control over their own lives, and some refuge against the unfriendly white city outside its borders. But the sad reality was that it remained badly overcrowded and desperately poor, with high illness and mortality rates; a high percentage of residents on relief; a high crime rate; inadequate recreational facilities; lack of building repairs; accumulated garbage and dirty streets; overcrowded schools; and high rates of police brutality.
>
> In white Chicago, the Great Migration produced a response that ranged from wariness to undisguised panic. The Chicago newspapers ran inflammatory headlines such as 'Half a Million Darkies from Dixie Swarm to the North to Better Themselves' and 'Negroes Arrive by Thousands — Peril to Health.' Articles in the city's three leading papers — the *Tribune*, the *Daily News*, and the *Herald Examiner* — generally overstated the size of the migration, and focused on the new arrivals' purported sickness, criminality, and vice.
>
> White Chicagoans worked to prevent the migrants from moving into white neighborhoods. One South Side neighborhood association captured the exclusionary spirit sweeping white Chicago when it declared that 'there is nothing in

the make-up of a Negro, physically or mentally, which should induce anyone to welcome him as a neighbor.'

In April 1917, the Chicago Real Estate Board met and — concerned about what officials described as the 'invasion of white residence districts by the Negroes' — appointed a Special Committee on Negro Housing to make recommendations. On this committee's recommendation, the board adopted a policy of block-by-block racial segregation, carefully controlled so that 'each block shall be filled solidly and. . . further expansion shall be confined to contiguous blocks.' Three years later, the board took the further step of voting unanimously to punish by 'immediate expulsion' any member who sold property to a black on a block where there were only white owners. (unk.)

George C. Adams early on was a Baptist and prominent in politics as a Republican, albeit, he ran as an Independent in the 1922 elections for Third Ward Alderman. Plus, he wrote a column, "Legal Hints," for the *Chicago Whip*.

According to the Encyclopedia of Chicago's website, "In the fall of 1929 the militant *Chicago Whip* foreshadowed later direct-action civil rights activism with its 'Spend Your Money Where You Can Work Campaign,' which targeted boycotts at chain stores that would serve but not hire blacks. The campaign registered some successes, pushing the number of black employees in stores in the black community to 25 percent and opening up approximately 100 white-collar jobs." (http://www.encyclopedia.chicagohistory.org, 2011)

The Great Depression slowed things down. In 1932, Papa surfaces again in newspapers after filing a lawsuit in the U. S. District Court against the Chicago Bell Telephone Co. for $15,000,000. The *Chicago Defender* headline read, "Telephone Co. Sued By Atty. George Adams – Claims City is Owed Over $15,000,000." (April 2, 1932) In 1934, he represents the Creek Tribe, of which his wife's grandmother is a member of, against the U. S. Government for a full accounting of all money due the National Council of Muskogee Indians. The *Chicago Defender* states that, "Washington, D. C. – The Muskogee (Creek) tribe of Indians of Beggs, Okla., last week filed a petition with Harold Ickes, Secretary of the Interior, demanding of the United States Government the sum of $150,000,000 which they claim was due them from Arkansas River Bed lands, and from the sale of surplus property belonging to the tribe. The Indians are represented by Sheridan

Bruseaux, special investigator, and George C. Adams, attorney." (March 21, 1942)

The thirties were the hey-day for my great-grandparents, especially my great-grandfather. He assumed a high stature in Chicago as he became more and more visible and outspoken. Both were constantly mentioned in the Chicago newspapers attending society, social, and sporting events. There are pictures of George with Joe Louis visiting Cook County Jail, and both of them at night clubs, galas, and big days at the horse/trotter races. Their popularity ended when Minerva was arrested in their home by a policewoman in the state's round-up of twenty so-called alleged fake spiritualists in March of 1939. The following month they filed a $100,000 suit against the *Chicago Herald and Examiner* for fraud, misrepresentation, and conspiracy. My understanding is that charges and both suits were dropped.

I do not find any social mention of them in the forties; only Attorney Adams is mentioned in cases, like the large suit mentioned earlier, and the fifties you know. It wasn't until the sixties that my two great-grandparents re-entered the social world and started re-appearing numerous times in society and business columns of newspapers. They held dinners, parties, soirees, and meetings. Even their birthday celebrations made the newspaper. They were both members and officers of the Oklahoma Club and Reverends with the Christian Science Invisible Church that gained notoriety for predicting John F. Kennedy's death. George was a member of the "Old Tymers" Club, the Howard University Chicago Alumni, and held office with the Grand Masons.

Papa was also a member of the Idlewilders, where his step-son, Siegel E. Young, Sr., was the President of the club for several years which helped to organize events and entertainment at the Idlewild Resort. Although they fought for integration, one of the most celebrated segregated Midwestern areas besides Bronzeville for Blacks was the Idlewild Resort in rural northwestern Michigan where Siegel II married my grandmother Lucille Clara.

Lake County, Michigan's website describes the city as:

> For four decades after its establishment in 1912, Idlewild was a rural retreat for African Americans seeking a bit of rest and relaxation outside the confines of their segregated communities in cities such as Detroit, Chicago, Indianapolis, and St. Louis. Referred to as 'Black Eden' at its peak, Idlewild was one of the

most popular resorts in the Midwest. Early lot owners included W.E.B. DuBois, founder of the NAACP. Dr. Daniel Williams of Chicago, the first person to perform open heart surgery (1893), also came to Idlewild for many years.

As many as 25,000 people would come in the height of the summer season to enjoy swimming, boating, fishing, hunting, camping, horseback riding, and nighttime entertainment. Count Basie, Sarah Vaughn, Billy Eckstine, Sammy Davis Jr., Della Reese, Bill Cosby, Louie Armstrong, Aretha Franklin, the Four Tops and many others were regulars at Idlewild's once-thriving nightspots. When the 1964 Civil Rights Act opened up other resorts to African-Americans, Idlewild's boomtown period subsided. (http://www.lakecountymichigan.com/idlewild, 2011)

Prof. Ben C. Wilson, co-author of *Black Eden: The Idlewild Community* wrote:

'I don't think there's any question that Idlewild was the foremost African American summer resort in the U.S. during the first half of the 20th century. If you wanted to watch major black entertainers or meet influential cultural figures during your vacation, this was the place to be.'

Opening in 1915, the sprawling lakeside resort became a vacationland for the elites of black society in Chicago, St. Louis, Detroit and New York. African American entertainers and artists performed for audiences that included black celebrities such as Joe Louis and pioneering Chicago heart surgeon Daniel Hale Williams.

But the Idlewild culture wasn't restricted to music. Over the years, many of the legendary 'Harlem Renaissance' artists and thinkers of the 1920s and 1930s, including novelist Zora Neale Hurston, poet Langston Hughes and scholar-activist W.E.B. DuBois, would gather here to trade ideas and gain inspiration. (2002)

Early on, like all young people George, or Papa, was very idealistic. He believed in the law and system as seen by his editorials and private papers. Because of the Cicero riot he lost faith in the system. His appearances in the paper immediately after the riot and years later were only for defending himself or testifying in court against principals from the riot. His business suffered but my great-grandmother kept him afloat because she had money, and the income from the buildings that they bought for themselves or someone in the family. After 1957 George went for the win and big settlement as he turned from general practice to criminal law to civil litigation. In 1960 he partnered with James Montgomery and Archie Watson.

In my research I came across an article written by George C. Adams which appeared in the *Chicago Defender* on June 1, 1935, as a response to an editorial in the column, "What People Say:"

> I quite agree with you that, 'No man is violating any law when he defends himself against a mob. Mobs are both cowardly and criminal at heart, 'If you must go then take somebody with you. Answer terror with terror; you can only die once.' There is a familiar quotation that there can be no remission of sin without the shedding of blood. Until the Negro learns to use his shotgun as was very diplomatically suggested in your editorial in a brave and fearless way for his own protection, anti-lynching laws would not accomplish very much for him if passed by the Congress of the United States.
>
> On or about March 4, 1909, a statute was passed by the Congress entitled, 'Offenses Against the Effective Franchise and Civil Rights.' As set forth in Barnes Federal Code, paragraph 9697 which reads as follows:
>
> > If two or more persons conspire to injure, oppress, threaten, or intimidate any citizen in the exercise or enjoyment of any right or privilege of the Constitution or laws of the U. S. or because of his having so exercised the same or if two or more persons go in disguise on the highway, or on the premises of another, with intent to prevent or hinder his free exercise or enjoyment of any right or privilege so secured, they shall be fined, not more than five thousand dollars and imprisoned not more than ten years, and shall, moreover, be thereafter ineligible to any office or place of honor, profit, or trust created by the Constitution or laws of the United States.
>
> Notwithstanding these statutes passed in 1909, providing for $5,000 fines and imprisonment not more than ten years, yet to date, as far as I know, no person has ever served one day or paid one fine for violating the statute. Neither has any great effort been made to enforce the same; therefore, what reason have we to believe that if the Costigan-Wagner Anti-Lynching Bill had succeeded in passage and had become a law that it would have been enforced any more than any other statute pertaining to

the depriving of citizens their rights under the present federal statute?

Atty. George C. Adams, 35 Dearborn St., Chicago, Ill. (unk.)

Chapter Ten
"'It Wasn't Us,' The Aftermath"

Mrs. De Rose's troubles continued. As my great-grandmother used to say, "Ugly is, as ugly does."
The Chicago Herald on June 13, 1952, wrote:
    Mrs. Camille De Rose, former owner of the Cicero Riot apartment building where mobs rioted last July was seized with a loaded revolver today during a trial in the Criminal courtroom of Judge Crowley.
    The jurist sentenced her to two years in the county jail for contempt of court.
    The red-haired, 44 yr-old women who was appearing against George C. Adams, her former attorney charged with embezzling two apartment buildings from her.
    Mrs. De Rose's sentencing followed a stormy hearing in which she claimed she is being persecuted by 'the South side bloc.'
    State's Attorney's Detectives seized a .32-caliber revolver containing four bullets from her briefcase after receiving a tip that she was, 'coming to court to shoot the judge.'
    Assistant State's Attorney James A. Brown was called this morning by the proprietor of a 63rd Street restaurant who said: 'Camille had breakfast here and said that she was going to shoot the judge and shoot up the court.'
    Detectives Waiting – Brown assigned Detective Ray Burton and Joseph Thurston to stand near Mrs. De Rose in the courtroom. Brown withheld his information from Judge Crowley to keep the Adams hearing free from prejudice.
    Soon after Brown and the detectives met Mrs. De Rose outside the courtroom.

When Brown told her that the hearing was being continued to June 26 because Adams' attorney was ill, Mrs. De Rose waved her briefcase overhead, shouted that she had received a telephone message about the attorney's illness and said she regarded this as a threat against her.

Brown persuaded her to enter the courtroom and she went before Judge Crowley flanked by detectives.

When Judge Crowley signified his willingness to grant Adams, who was not present, another continuance, Mrs. De Rose banged the briefcase on a table and shouted: 'I am being dragged around by the Southside bloc. First it was the Cicero syndicate and now it's this. Adams is famous for dragging his cases. I want justice and I'm going to get it somewhere. I'm not going to be made a goat.'

Judge Crowley interrupted to say, 'You'd better stop talking.'

Order Removal – Then he directed bailiffs to remove Mrs. De Rose to the bullpen, indicating that he intended to punish her for contempt of court.

In an anteroom, where she continued babbling to the point of hysteria, her case was searched and the revolver found.

Forty-five minutes later she was recalled before Judge Crowley who waited until she was seated in the witness box and then asked her: 'Why did you bring a gun into this courtroom?'

'Because I have been threatened constantly,' she replied hotly adding, 'Why should I be put on trial? Adams said that he would defeat me mentally, physically, and financially. I have asked the FBI to protect my home at 6336 S. Drexel Av.'

Here her attorney, Aaron Payne, interceded, explaining that she suffered 'much anguish' since the rioting and the loss of her property.

Judge Crowley stated: 'This is perhaps true but it is not the issue. The issue is that she came into this court prepared to take the law into her own hands. The clerk will prepare an order for a sentence of one year in the county jail for direct contempt of this court.' (p. 1, #293, pm ed.)

Who lets a known armed gunman into a courtroom? Furthermore I'm sure Illinois statute for illegally caring a concealed weapon had a larger sentence.

Camille wrote as her defense for carrying the gun, "The decree in Judge Haas' court which Attorney Payne put over by sending me to the State's Attorney's office. The decree failed to mention the $4,750.00 oil swindle, and provided for the sale of my building, against my will, and to pay 7 ½ % of the proceeds to a Jewel Young, said to be the grand-niece of or something of George C. Adams. It was that provision which sent up my blood pressure to bursting and I reached for a gun." (p. 339)

As you can see again, there is some disparity in the details. The newspaper mentioned that the gun stayed in her briefcase all of the time, but Camille claims that she was going to pull it out or had taken it out.

The reality of it was that from what I was told, my great-grandparents and father agreed to call about Camille carrying the gun because she threatened to shoot them, as well as singling out my aunt. The restaurant owner was tipped. It is interesting how this information was handled by the State's Attorney. Of course, nothing connected with the Cicero incident made much sense. Common practice on the south side of Chicago if you really needed help you told the police that the crime was being committed against a white person. If you were in grave or life-threatening trouble, one practice that my great-grandmother advocated was to tell the police that a white woman was being raped. As her dementia progressed she even used this line on my uncle who was trying to get her home, and the police took them both in.

Camille made no qualms of showing her dislike for my family. "The chief defendant in the foreclosure is the same Jewel Young, who fraudulently holds the title to my building, for which she paid nothing, and for which Adams paid nothing. Before I can even attempt to redeem my building I must get rid of Jewel Young. To do so I must have the fraudulent decree set aside by Judge Haas." (p. 339)

What Ms. De Rose did not understand is that being black is not a condition or fashion statement that you can get rid of or take off when not convenient. Whether life treats you fairly or not, "black" can't be disrobed. This epiphany never took place for her because she was seen as a woman, not a white woman, and no matter how un-fair, the first thing distinguished with an African-American regardless of hue was that he or she was a black woman or black man, not woman or man.

Let's see how many criminal charges (5) were brought against my family?

1. Conspiracy to depreciate real estate
2. Conspiracy to incite a riot
3. Conspiracy to damage property
4. Embezzlement
5. Violation of her rights, Petition by C. De Rose

Let's see how many civil charges (3) were brought against my family? They were:
1. Fraud,
2. Disbarment, and
3. Challenge against award on suit.

Only one criminal suit filed on behalf of my family (Edwards, Minerva Adams) along with the Clarks, and the Scotts in June 1951 was for violation of Civil Rights for $200,000 by NAACP.

How many charges were brought against the mob of 118 that were arrested? Almost all the rioters were freed that night or the next day with no bail. The ones who did nothing wrong, (Adams, Edwards, Clarks) were released if they posted their bail set at $5,000.

Crowds on the day of the move (Adams, G.)

Cicero Officials' crimes under statute should have resulted in fines up to $5,000 and up to ten years imprisonment for rioting. The

Cook County Grand Jury failed to indict the rioters but instead chose to indict the victims of: Violation of Civil Rights Statute and Conspiracy in Connection With the Riot. Camille filed three civil suits; the Clarks filed three separate suits; my great-grandfather filed one individually; and my father filed none.

Let's look at the case of Police Chief Erwin Konovsky, and his policemen aides: Sgt. Roland Brani and Officer Frank Lange who were finally indicted by a federal grand jury for malfeasance for failing to do their duty. They were found guilty by Judge Walter LaBuy on June 23, 1952, and Konovsky was fined $2,000, and his aides were fined $250; although, they did not pay pending an appeal.

Judge LaBuy in his decision further expounded on the cause of such action according to the *Chicago Tribune* of June 24, 1952, "'This event did not originate on account of altruistic desires to obtain homes to relieve the over-crowded living conditions of Negroes.' Calls Motives Revenge - 'Rather, its inception stemmed from the revengeful motives of a landlady in difficulty with her tenants and the avaricious scheme of her attorney to obtain an unconscionable profit on the apartment building under threats of renting the apartments to Negroes. It was the reprehensible plotting of the landlady and her attorney which culminated in this most unfortunate occurrence.'" (p. 1)

The three policemen filed an appeal and the U. S. Appellate Court reversed the verdict and sentence on March 9, 1953; in December 1954 Judge Sam Perry cleared them of conspiracy. This was after the mayor, town attorney, and fire marshal were cleared several months earlier.

Crowds before the Cicero Riot (Adams, G.)

The 118 rioters and two others arrested who were released without bond the night of the riot or the next morning appeared in court before Magistrate Capouch in October of 1951 on the following dates: 3rd – 3 were freed; 2 fined $10; 18 failed to appear; 5th – 49 rioters were freed because a representative from the National Guard did not show that day to testify. 9 men were fined $10; 1 paid $25; and 13th – 12 were fined $149; 44 were freed on a technicality.

On Sept 18th, the Cook County Grand Jury indicted six people, albeit Cicero Police Chief Ed Konovsky was indicted separately from the remaining five: Camille De Rose, George Adams, Charles S. Edwards, Norman Silverman, and George Leighton (who wasn't even in town at the time of the incident) to appear Oct. 9th. The last five were held for $5,000 bond, and the Chief was let go on "his own recognizance." Respectable citizens who really committed no crime without criminal records, save Mrs. De Rose, had to post bond but rioters did not. Early on my great-grandfather represented the Clarks; later on the NAACP and other lawyers took over.

My great-grandfather posted his bail. My father was not there at the time and a warrant was issued. When he turned himself in with my great-grandfather as his lawyer who introduced evidence of why he could not appear. My great-grandfather paid Dad's $500; this is why my great-grandfather kept the eventual settlement of the civil rights suit in 1957 for $300.

According to *Time Magazine* on October 10, 1951:

'Sequels worse than the Cicero Riots,' Edmund Burke said that he did not know how to indict a whole people; but last week the Cook County, Ill. Grand Jury found a way of misusing the power of indictment to disgrace a whole metropolis.

The Grand Jury investigated the riots at Cicero, an all-white town, where Harvey E. Clark, a Negro, was prevented from moving into an apartment that he had rented. (*Time*, July 23). Not one of the 126 persons arrested for rioting was indicted. Instead the Grand Jury indicted George C. Adams, a Negro, who is part owner of the building where Clark leased the home; Charles Edwards, a Negro rental agent who handled the deal, and George Leighton, a respected Negro lawyer who acted as attorney for Clark and for the National Association for the Advancement of Colored People after the riots started . . .

The three Negroes, Leighton, Edwards, and Adams, are accused of 'conspiracy to damage property.' The Grand Jury seems to think that it is wrong to rent an apartment in Cicero to a Negro, wrong to defend his rights, but O.K. to burn his furniture and chase him out of town. (unk.)

The town of Cicero rounded up witnesses that testified that my family (Edwards & Adams) had conspired to steal the property at 6319 W. 19th St., and start a riot for their own gain, not even to promote Civil Rights. No one would, and certainly they did not.

Moreover, to further incite the people in the metro area of Chicago and denigrate the good name and image of my father and great-grandfather the Grand Jury added in Norman Silverman, who just happened to be someone who showed up on television, as this was the first time a riot was televised. Silverman was unconnected with any of the principals or anything. He was a convenient patsy because he was a known Communist Activist. So being colored wasn't enough they had to also be Communist. What's more the signs in court and around the town of Cicero exacerbated this notion once they found out that my great-grandfather was colored, "Race Mixing is Communist."

The supercilious part of the indictment was to include George Leighton who did not know any of the principals until June 8th. By including Attorney Leighton of the NAACP and unknown diverse others this helped to further the conspiracy theory of a pre-meditated act of violence on a national scale.

The full transcript of the indictment is more insidious to Chicago where most of the Grand Jury members came from as much as it is to Cicero. The full indictment reads of September 18, 1951, State of Illinois, County of Cook SS:

Of the extended July term of the Criminal Court of Cook County, in said county and state, in the year of our Lord one thousand nine hundred fifty-one.

The Grand Jurors chosen, selected and sworn, in and for the County of Cook, in the State of Illinois, for July, A. D. 1951 term, said Grand Jury having been continued in existence and its term further extended for thirty days on the thirty first of August, A. D. 1951, according to law, in the name and by the authority of the People of the State of Illinois, upon their oaths present that one CAMILLE DE ROSE, one GEORGE C. ADAMS, one GEORGE LEIGHTON, one CHARLES EDWARDS and one NORMAN SILVERMAN, late of the Cook County of Illinois on the thirteenth day of July in the year of our Lord one thousand nine hundred fifty-one, in said County of Cook, in the State of Illinois aforesaid, unlawfully, maliciously, and willfully conspired, combined, confederated, and agreed together with each other and with divers other persons whose names are unknown to said Grand Jurors, with fraudulent and malicious intent unlawfully, wrongfully and wickedly to injure the property of a large number of other persons the exact number of whom and the names of whom are unknown to Grand Jurors, with the fraudulent and malicious intent unlawfully, wrongfully and wickedly to injure the property of a large number of other persons the exact number of whom and the names of whom are unknown to said Grand Jurors but who constituted a group and class and were representative owners of a large number of divers parcels of real property, being the owners of real property in a residential section of the Town of Cicero, Cook County, Illinois, in the general vicinity of a certain apartment building commonly known as number Six Thousand One Hundred Thirty Nine West Nineteenth Street in said town of Cicero, of which GEORGE C.

ADAMS then was the owner and the sole beneficiary under a certain trust agreement known as number 13229, with LaSalle National Bank, a national bank association at Chicago, Illinois, covering the ownership of said building; that is to say, maliciously and willfully to cause a depreciation in the market selling price of, and the income to the respective owners through rental of, said parcels of real property by renting and causing to be rented a certain apartment in said building to Harvey Clark and Johnette Clark and inducing, aiding and encouraging said Harvey Clark and Johnette Clark to move into said apartment and reside there and move their belongings and personal effects into said apartment, when certain persons in said town objected to said Harvey Clark and Johnette Clark objected to their residing in said apartment building;

And further, by unlawfully, willfully, and maliciously inciting, persuading and encouraging a large number, to-wit: about three thousand of people, some of whom where armed with stones, bricks and divers other dangerous weapons, unlawfully, riotously and tumultuously to assemble around and in said apartment building for the purpose of disturbing the public peace and creating a riot there and doing unlawful acts, with force and violence, against personal property, goods and chattels of said Harvey Clark and Johnetta Clark then being in said apartment; to-wit: unlawfully, willfully and maliciously destroying, injuring and secreting the household furniture, piano, clothing, jewelry and personal effects of said Harvey Clark and Johnetta Clark then in said apartment by throwing said household furniture, piano, jewelry, clothing and personal effects out from the windows of an upper story, to-wit: the third floor, of said building down onto the sidewalk and the street below and by breaking and treating said effects and clothing without said rioters then and there having the consent of said Harvey Clark and Johnette Clark or of either of them; and for the purpose of doing unlawful acts, with force and violence against said building to-wit, unlawfully, willfully and maliciously injuring and defacing said building and divers fixtures therein by throwing divers large stones and bricks at and against said building and at and through the windows of said building, thereby defacing the façade of said building and breaking said windows and breaking and defacing inside walls, plaster and floors of said building, and by knocking over and breaking divers refrigerators, radiators, stoves, faucets, sinks, wash bowls, toilets and electric light fixtures all of which then and there were fixtures in said building, without said rioters then and there having consent of said George C. Adams;

and, further, by unlawfully, willfully and maliciously insisting, persuading, and encouraging said rioters, when they where commended in the name of the State of Illinois, by police officers of said town and by the sheriff and deputy sheriffs of said county who were present at the scene of said riot, immediately and peaceably to disperse, to neglect and refuse to disperse without unnecessary delay, but on the contrary to remain present at the scene of said riot and continue to riot and continue to injure and deface said building and fixtures;

And, further by unlawfully, willfully and maliciously inciting, persuading, and encouraging said rioters so assembled to threaten to continue and repeat said rioting in case said Harvey Clark and Johnetta Clark were permitted to reside in said apartment building or reside in said Town of Cicero;

And all the matters aforesaid then and there had a tendency to cause said section of town of Cicero to be considered an unsafe and undesirable place of residence and said parcels of real property to be considered undesirable property for the purposes of ownership, residence, and leasing to others, and therefore had a tendency to injure said parcels of real property and to cause such depreciation in the market selling price of, and the income to the respective owners through rental of, said parcels of real property;

contrary to the Statute, and against the peace and dignity of the same People of the State of Illinois.

Count 2. The Grand Jurors aforesaid, chosen, selected and sworn, in and for the County of Cook, in the State of Illinois, in the name and by the authority of the People of the State of Illinois, upon their oaths aforesaid, do further present that one

Camille de Rose, one George C. Adams, one George Leighton, one Charles Edwards and one Norman Silverman, late of the Cook County of Illinois on the thirteenth day of July in the year of our Lord one thousand nine hundred fifty-one, in said County of Cook , in the State of Illinois aforesaid, unlawfully, maliciously, and willfully conspired, combined, confederated, and agreed together with each other and with divers other persons whose names are unknown to said Grand Jurors, unlawfully, willfully, wrongfully, fraudulently and maliciously to cause financial damage and loss to a large number of other persons the exact number of whom and the names of whom are unknown to said Grand Jurors but who constituted a group and class, and were the respective owners of a large number of divers parcels of real property, being the owners of real property in a residential section of the town of Cicero, Cook County, Illinois, in the general vicinity of a certain apartment building commonly known as number Six Thousand One Hundred Thirty Nine West Nineteenth Street in said town of Cicero, of which said George C. Adams then was the owner and the sole beneficiary under a certain trust agreement known as number 13229, with LaSalle National Bank, a national banking association at Chicago, Illinois, covering the ownership of said building;

that is to say, maliciously and willfully to cause a depreciation in the market selling price of, and the income to the respective owners through rental of, said parcels of real property,

by renting and causing to be rented a certain apartment in said building to Harvey Clark and Johnette Clark and inducing aiding and encouraging said Harvey Clark and Johnette Clark to move into said apartment and reside there and move their belongings and reside there and move their belongings and personal effects into said apartment, when certain persons in said town objected to said Harvey Clark and Johnette Clark objected to their residing in said apartment building;

and further, by unlawfully, willfully, and maliciously inciting, persuading and encouraging a large number, to-wit: about three thousand of people, some of whom where armed with stones, bricks and divers other dangerous weapons, unlawfully, riotously and tumultuously to assemble around and in said apartment building for the purpose of disturbing the public peace and creating a riot there and doing unlawful acts, with force and violence, against personal property, goods and chattels of said Harvey Clark and Johnetta Clark then being in said apartment; to-wit: unlawfully, willfully and maliciously destroying, injuring and secreting the household furniture, piano, clothing, jewelry and personal effects of said Harvey Clark and Johnetta Clark then in said apartment by throwing said household furniture, piano, jewelry, clothing and personal effects out from the windows of an upper story, to-wit: the third floor, of said building down onto the sidewalk and the street below and by breaking and treating said effects and clothing without said rioters then and there having the consent of said Harvey Clark and Johnette Clark or of either of them; and for the purpose of doing unlawful acts, with force and violence against said building to-wit, unlawfully, willfully and maliciously injuring and defacing said building and divers fixtures therein by throwing divers large stones and bricks at and against said building and at and through the windows of said building, thereby defacing the façade of said building and breaking said windows and breaking and defacing inside walls, plaster and floors of said building, and by knocking over and breaking divers refrigerators, radiators, stoves, faucets, sinks, wash bowls, toilets and electric light fixtures all of which then and there were fixtures in said building, without said rioters then and there having consent of said George C. Adams;

And, further, by unlawfully, willfully and maliciously insisting, persuading, and encouraging said rioters, when they where commanded in the name of the State of Illinois, by police officers of said town and by the sheriff and deputy sheriffs of said county who were present at the scene of said riot, immediately and peaceably to disperse, to neglect and refuse to disperse without unnecessary delay, but on the contrary to remain present at the scene of said riot and continue to riot and continue to injure and deface said building and fixtures;

and, further by unlawfully, willfully and maliciously inciting, persuading, and encouraging said rioters so assembled to threaten to continue and repeat said rioting in case said Harvey Clark and Johnetta Clark were permitted to reside in said apartment building or reside in said Town of Cicero;

and that all the matters aforesaid then and there had a tendency to cause said section of town of Cicero to be considered an unsafe and undesirable place of residence and said parcels of real property to be considered undesirable property for the purposes of ownership, residence, and leasing to others, and therefore had a tendency to injure said parcels of real property and to cause such depreciation in the market, selling price of and the income to the respective owners through rental of, said parcels of real property, and had a tendency to cause financial damage and loss to the owners of said parcels of real property

contrary to the Statute, and against the peace and dignity of the same People of the State of Illinois.

Count 3. The Grand Jurors aforesaid, chosen, selected and sworn, in and for the County of Cook, in the State of Illinois, in the name and by the authority of the People of the State of Illinois, upon their oaths aforesaid, do further present that one

Camille de Rose, one George C. Adams, one George Leighton, one Charles Edwards and one Norman Silverman, late of the Cook County of Illinois on the thirteenth day of July in the year of our Lord one thousand nine hundred fifty-one, in said County of Cook , in the State of Illinois aforesaid, unlawfully, maliciously, and willfully conspired, combined, confederated, and agreed together with each other and with divers other persons whose names are unknown to said Grand Jurors, unlawfully, willfully, wrongfully, wickedly and maliciously to incite, persuade and encourage a large number, to-wit: about three thousand, of people, some of whom where armed with stones, bricks and divers other dangerous weapons, unlawfully, riotously and tumultuously to assemble around and in a certain apartment building commonly known as number Six Thousand One Hundred Thirty Nine West Nineteenth Street in the Town of Cicero, Cook County, Illinois (of which said George C. Adams then was the owner and the sole beneficiary under a certain trust agreement known as number 13229, with LaSalle National Bank, a national banking association at Chicago, Illinois, covering the ownership of said building,) for the purpose of disturbing the peace and creating a riot there and doing unlawful acts with force and violence, against personal property, goods and chattels of said Harvey Clark and Johnette Clark which then and there were in said building, to wit: unlawfully, willfully and maliciously destroying, injuring and secreting the household furniture, piano, clothing, jewelry and personal effects of said Harvey Clark and Johnette Clark then in said building by throwing said household furniture, piano, jewelry, clothing and personal effects out from the windows of an upper story, to-wit:

the third floor, of said building down onto the sidewalk and the street below and by breaking and treating said effects and clothing without said rioters then and there having the consent of said Harvey Clark and Johnette Clark or of either of them; and for the purpose of doing unlawful acts, with force and violence against said building, to-wit: unlawfully, willfully and maliciously injuring and defacing said building and divers fixtures therein by throwing divers large stones and bricks at and against said building and at and through the windows of said building, thereby defacing the façade of said building and breaking said windows and breaking and defacing inside walls, plaster and floors of said building, and by knocking over and breaking divers refrigerators, radiators, stoves, faucets, sinks, wash bowls, toilets and electric light fixtures all of which then and there were fixtures in said building, without said rioters then and there having consent of said George C. Adams;

and, further, by unlawfully, wrongfully, wickedly and maliciously to incite, persuade and encourage said rioters, when they where commanded in the name of the State of Illinois, by police officers of said town and by the sheriff and deputy sheriffs of said county who were present at the scene of said riot, immediately and peaceably to disperse, to neglect and refuse to disperse without unnecessary delay, but on the contrary to remain present at the scene of said riot and continue to riot and continue to injure and destroy said personal property, goods and chattels and continue to injure and deface said building and fixtures;

and, further, by unlawfully, wrongfully, wickedly and maliciously to incite, persuade and encourage said rioters so assembled to threaten to continue and repeat said rioting; contrary to the Law and against the peace and dignity of the same People of the State of Illinois. [Errors which occurred in the original document were kept.]

John S. Boyle, States Attorney

Well, there is very little to be said about such an inane document. I smiled and shook my head through every adverb, adjective and adverb of the adverb about conniving Negroes. States Attorney John Boyle and his several lawyers had the most warped, fictional version of what took place, and what democracy should be. Mysterious people of the town did not want you to live in their town, so by moving into their town, you broke the law. Furthermore, you should not have planned a riot where a mob of 3,000 came with or found weapons and attacked you, or came out to burn your property because unknown people got hurt and things were destroyed.

The real conspiracy should have been with the town, its officers, et al. and the other 19 tenants who mysteriously had moved out. Did they have an inkling that something might happen or a spiritualist told them if they didn't move by July 11th something might happen? How was it that most of the building was empty and only, "The household furniture, piano, clothing, jewelry and personal effects of said Harvey Clark and Johnetta Clark" were damaged when the building burned? Ms. De Rose received payment for burned furniture she sold my great-grandfather and for the rest that was moved to her new apartment. Why wasn't anyone else mentioned in the indictment, like any of the 118 rioters other than Silverman? Actually had this been thought out better, or a better prepared statement with names and addresses used the State's Attorney might have had a case.

Damages to the burned building and furniture after the riot (Edwards, C.)

This farce of justice was even believed by the members of the Grand Jury. As the members left, the *Chicago Tribune* got two statements on September 26, 1951, the first by Mrs. William Mann, "'We did our job conscientiously and with our best judgment. This was the finest group of its kind assembled in this county.' James A. Brown, assistant state's attorney who assisted the grand jury, pointed out that the jury heard 70 witnesses and was in session nearly 100 hours. He described the grand jury as the most independent one in his 21 years' experience. He was asked why none of the actual rioters was indicted. 'I know why,' he said, 'but I cannot comment on what goes on in the grand jury room.'" (Sept. 27, 1951, p. C5)

My comment would be that this had more to do with race. It was bad enough that the hard-working Clarks wanted to move into an all-white suburb of Chicago, but then you had the "Uppity Negroes" who were lawyers and owned their own businesses who had bought white owned property as they had done in Hyde Park-Kenwood and turned it over to Negroes. They had to be punished.

Each of the three counts carried a sentence of 1 to 5 years or a $5,000 fine, or both. *The Tribune* reported that, First Assistant State's Attorney Breen said, "'The Grand Jury of 23 persons has heard a lot of evidence in this case'. . .Attorney Adams said, 'It's the worst thing I ever heard of a Grand Jury. That we conspired to lower property values and stir up a riot, as the indictment charges, is ridiculous. I had the absolute right to rent the property to anybody. The Supreme Court has thrown out restrictive covenants. A Negro can rent property anywhere. We might as well tear up the Constitution if such rights are denied. Fifteen million Negroes will resent the grand jury's charges,' said Adams." (unk.)

No bills were returned against my great-grandmother, rioters, Cicero officials or policemen, or the Cook County Sheriff and his deputies, or Joseph Beauharnais, President of the White Circle League passing out pamphlets, which according to the State's Attorney and the Police Chief were illegal without permission. So did Beauharnais have permission or Cicero officials turned the other way?

The first two counts on "The Negroes" were thrown out by the Judge; argued by a mere technicality of ambiguity. My father shows in his notes to Attorney Joe Clayton who represented my father and great-grandfather in this particular case, that vicinity is a vague term. Upon conferring with my great-grandfather and presenting it in argument the first two counts of conspiracy were quashed.

Dad's courtroom notes read:

Question constitutionality, grant of authority and limitation of authority, [that these items and accusations] set forth basis for first condemnation not for second except in vague terms. There is no description of property and use delimitating terms [when speaking of class/groups of people], i.e. 1st class of people; tendencies are not within the purview of the criminal statute. General vicinity does not mean 'Semi-circle.'" My father cited the following legal precedents in the margins, "US v. Johnson 319 U.S. 63 – does not set out in sufficient particularly the offense charges. . . 'If means is unlawful they must set forth in sufficient particularity, re: certain persons.' (311 Ill). – 'Cannot set off certain class or group of people in sufficient particularity,' count 1 statute, count 2 common law, count 3 – where did acts take place to incite the mob?

His notes continued on the back of the indictment:

Robert Ming, representing De Rose, 1) authority vague, 2) adjectives ---? ----. . .Thurgood Marshall argues for Leighton. . . Objecting parties have no standing in court; right to acquire and use property & certain persons objected, Buchannan B. Wyley. (245 U. S. 60); racial restrictive covenants, Shelley v. Kraemer, Sykes v. McGlee, Hurst v. Hodge (334 U. S. 1, 63 U. S. 836), Slaughter v. Virginia: state can not through its judicial system preclude a person from occupying prop. because of race.

Another column of notes read:

Nothing in indictment shows: 1) why they objected, 2) right to object, 3) that they were lawful abiding people. Ex partie laws, (93 p. 2d 74). Indictment alleged to protect property rights of unknown people; property rights being ignored are rights of Clarks. Using state machinery through criminal action to do what could not be done in the civil courts: 1) ordinances, 2) restrictive agreements, 30 indictments (?).

Another panel reads:

Miss Hart – basis of count. 1, sect. 139 – 'injuring the property of another could not plead in bar to future indictments. Counts 1 & 2 relate to 'tendency;' statute does not. Special legislation counties of 500,000 or more refers to only one county – Cook. Hunt v. County of Cook (398 Ill 412) People ex. Rel. (405 Ill 511); compelling point: vagueness and failure to inform defendants of what they are charged.

The last note reads:

Joe Clayton – conspiracy 2 or more persons. To do unlawful act or to do lawful act by unlawful means; 13th day of July; (339 Ill. 543) Lowry v. People. Conspiracy to induce Clarks to move in. Indictment says these people including the owner conspired. Did Clarks have right to rent or move in? Does not set forth actionable conspiracy. Must show by facts set forth in indictment that it was unlawful for Clarks to move in. (1952)

Several months later the outcome of the remaining one count ended in no decision. The case may have ended but the terrorization directed at my family had only just begun. No arrests or charges, according to my father, were ever made on anyone who had physically or verbally attacked them or people connected with them.

Many continuances and years later the $200,000 civil suit was settled on the 5th of April, 1957, by Judge Knoch. Each person: Minerva Adams, Charles Edwards, and the Scotts, Maurice Sr. & Jr., received $300 each. What a travesty of justice!

Another conspiracy theory was set in motion by a Cicero real estate dealer by the name of Frank Broz. He claimed that the owners of 6319 19th St., in Cicero, Ms. De Rose, my great-grandfather, and my aunt, precipitated the riot by trying to sell the building at a marked up price.

Mr. Broz and his backers later said that the asking price of $140,000 was too much for them. He thought property price should be only $110,000, based on the twenty apartments rent of $1,098 by a multiple of 3-4. (Adams, 1951)

Mr. Broz started making calls and talking to the press when he found out that Ms. De Rose had not only sold the building out from under him but sold it to Negroes! My thoughts are that Broz, et al. were surprised to hear that De Rose had sold her building, and extremely shocked to find out that Coloreds now owned it, so he gave press interviews and talked to city officials. He was instrumental in getting the three indictments of conspiracy: conspiracy to damage property in the vicinity, conspiracy to incite a riot and, especially the one to lower the value of property in the vicinity.

Broz, like Ms. De Rose, claimed that the Clarks were duped. This time he claims that the Clarks were merely a tool.

Early on articles naming my family members just listed their name and title, e. g. "Charles Edwards, Real Estate Broker and George Adams, Attorney." In the midst of the incident they were captioned as,

"Charles Edwards, real estate broker that rented the apartment to the Clarks," and "George Adams, Attorney for Camille De Rose." After the riots, my father was now captioned as, "Charles Edwards, Negro, real estate broker that rented the apartment to the Clarks" and my great-grandfather was, "George C. Adams, Negro, Attorney for Camille De Rose." Things even got so bad that instead of the customary Attorney George C. Adams; it would just be, "George C. Adams, Negro," or instead of, "Real Estate Broker, Negro," it finally became, "Charles Edwards, Negro." One would think from articles that "Negro" was their last name or their claim to fame. Yes, that was exactly the gist of it!

It's amazing how color was bantered about when there needed to be an alarm buzzed. Broz continued vacillating about his own color conspiracy in regards to the riot that Camille by having tenants pay at a Negro Attorney's office in February 1951, and then using a Negro collector was using their race as a threat to get the tenants to pay higher rents. The repartee was because you are paying to Negroes this would elevate fears and help with your purported scheme by using race.

Camille De Rose who changed her allegiance by the day and who was sought out for by warrants that mysteriously were dropped was now testifying against the very people she said were for her. Ms. De Rose claims that every lawyer took advantage of her: Adams, Berwyn attorney, Keys, Leighton, Payne, Berkos, D'Angelo, Fine, Rosin, Porto, Love, et al, plus Judges, administrators, and especially the Cicero town officials.

Yet, here she was testifying on their behalf and lying, too. She admitted in deposition to the States Attorney that she was in collusion with the Negroes in scheming to use race as a means to increase her rents and the selling of her building. Furthermore, she and her lawyer at the time, Adams, plotted to get a high selling price and split the profits. (De Rose)

Camille in her autobiography and the *Chicago Tribune* have two different accounts about what happened; Camille in her book says that my great-grandfather just took over the building. Now, in deposition the building was to be a co-op. In Camille's testimony as reported by the *Tribune*, one can see how much the two Assistant States Attorneys directed her in questioning and led her into seemingly rehearsed answers:

The inquiry by attorneys Goldstein and Flood continued,
'Q - Did Adams tell you he could get $170,000 for the building?

A- Yes. Q – Did he tell you how he would get the money? A – No. He said just leave it to him. He would make more than that much. Q – As a matter of fact, he told you that when it was learned the building was bought by colored people, the tenants and civic people of Cicero would get so scared and frightened that he could get practically any offer? A – Yes. Q – And as a consequence of the plan, Adams himself went out to the building during January, February, and March? A- Yes. '

Several factors are not true. Camille in many sources states that during this period that she thought Papa was white. Trust me, no one in the building would have ascertained any thing else. As a matter of fact even Cicero officials (Town Attorney, Director of Rent Control, and Police Chief) thought he was white until told differently when Camille told them after meeting his family, and later they started investigating Papa and my father. Camille was only concerned about her own well-being since she was having, "Domestic troubles," (p. 110) and money troubles by the way of decontrolled rents. She met Papa when she hired him to fight the Cicero Office of Rent Control in March 1951 after meeting only a month earlier.

The deposition continues:

'Q – Did he tell you why he wanted a colored family to move into the flat? A – He said he would get his price and show the town of Cicero about decontrolled rents. He told me that they had taken away my constitutional rights . . . She said that she agreed to move out April 1st so that Harvey E. Clark, Negro bus driver, and his wife could take her apartment. After the riot, she said Adams came to her and wanted $30,000 to protect her interests. She said she would get another lawyer, and would also go to the police. 'That won't do you any good,' she related he said. 'I fixed this thing: I planned this thing and I have lived with it. You're not going to tell anything. I'll have them put you away as insane. . . You'll go to prison or be locked up as insane.' Boyle said the deposition would be used in fighting Mrs. De Rose's suit against the County. (*Chicago Tribune*, March 14, 1952, p. 13)

Next, Camille states in her book that apartment C2 originally housed the Pratts who moved into a basement apartment because of money and an aging mother. Someone told her she could get more money by furnishing the apartment which she did without living there initially. When her domestic issues got worse she moved in briefly; however, financial issues superseded this and she needed the money or in this case extra money because "C2" now no longer fell under rent control. The Clarks did not come to know my father or great-grandfather or anything about the apartment until June.

Secondly, Harvey Clark was not the first to view the apartment; four others viewed it besides him. Harvey Clark stopped by Illinois Realty on June 6, 1951, at 1 pm in response to my father's ad viewing the property on the 7th and planning to move on the 8th. Camille even says that my father came out initially to see about renting the apartment. This is definitely a lie because my father had just bought a building in his company's name were he, my mother, and siblings lived. They were close to other family members and his office. They were not moving to Cicero. There wasn't even a thought of moving, as stated recently by both parents. The sad thing is that she thought that she was getting back at my great-grandfather and father. The police and states attorney played her. They in turn used the same testimony to win a judgment against her in her suit against the county. Camille got herself locked up as insane; there was nothing fixed except her testimony.

Broz who also testified was key to spreading the rumors about Norman Silverman being a communist sympathizer. I'm surprised this wasn't thrown in sooner with the new era of McCarthyism.

The Chicago Tribune in their article, "Riot Jury Told of Dual Role of Agitator" reported on the Grand Jury testimony on August 15, 1951, that Norman Silverman, 26 (They did not say Norman Silverman, White or Jewish.) of 8001 Edgewater Rd., Riverside, IL, "Robert Holocek, Cicero policeman, reportedly identified Silverman to jurors as the man he saw urging the mob to action . . . Silverman was wearing a button, 'Go, Go, Keep Cicero White.'" Another policeman testified on August 7th, that Silverman, with an Eva Terveen a. k. a. Eva Young, was passing out handbills illegally and was arrested. They could not produce the flyer but could bring in witnesses. (Aug. 15, 1951, p. 13) If you riot because a Negro family is moving in wouldn't you be more upset at knowing that Negroes owned the building in the neighborhood? Unfortunately those who were rioting did not have privy to all of the information, because if they did, they wouldn't have just burned the one apartment that was rented by Negroes, instead they would have burned down the whole Negro owned building.

The second agitator, who was by far worse than Silverman who was just unlucky, was Joseph Beauharnais. The journalist who was in the front seat of my father's car when Konovsky put the gun to his head wrote for the *Pittsburgh Courier*. Beauharnais was the one agitating the mob; however, he was never indicted or prosecuted. It was believed that he was welcomed by the town of Cicero and ignored in any court cases or depositions because some were members along with Beauharnais in the White Circle League. One of the writer's most poignant articles came on July 5, 1952, with a photo of Beauharnais titled "What's Behind the Cicero Riot?" Beauharnais later sued the paper for libel. The case (243 F.2d 705) was heard and then appealed before the U. S. Court of Appeals Seventh Circuit on April 19, 1957, by Chief Judge Duffy, and Judges Finnegan and Swain. Excerpts of the decision are as follows:

Plaintiff's complaint herein sought damages from defendant for publishing alleged libelous matter in the January 5, 1952, issue of its newspaper, *The Pittsburgh Courier*. Defendant is a Pennsylvania corporation, and plaintiff a resident of Illinois. Jurisdiction was based upon diversity of citizenship. The record indicates defendant's newspaper is circulated principally among members of the colored race.

Defendant published in its January 5, 1952 issue an article with a large headline 'What's Behind the Cicero Riot?' Plaintiff's photograph appeared as part of the background for the headline. Also, as part of said background, was reproduced a circular or pamphlet with the heading 'The White Circle League of America', which listed plaintiff as the founder. The circular was worded as follows:

'The White Circle League of America' Founder-- Joseph Beauharnais P.O. Box 531-- Chicago 90, Illinois 'Dedicated to protect and maintain the Dignity, Social Edicts, Customs and rights of the White Race in America. 'Wanted' One Million Self Respecting White People in Chicago to Unite under the Banner of the White Circle League of America to oppose the National Campaign now on and supported by Truman's Infamous Civil Rights Program and some Church Organizations to amalgamate the black and white races with the object of mongrelizing the white race.

The White Circle League of America is the only articulate white voice in America being raised in protest against Negro aggressions and infiltrations into all white neighborhoods. The white people of Chicago Must take advantage of this opportunity to become united. If persuasion and the need to prevent the white race from becoming mongrelized by the Negro will not unite us, then the aggressions * * * rapes, robberies, knives, guns and marijuana of the Negro, Surely Will.

The Negro has many national organizations working to push him into the midst of the white people on many fronts. The white race does not have a single organization to work on a National Scale to make its wishes articulate and to assert its natural rights to self-preservation. The White Circle League of America proposes to do the job.

I wish to be enrolled as a member in The White Circle League of America, and I will do my best to secure ten or more members. Joseph Beauharnais.'

The words of the article of which plaintiff complained and set forth in his complaint are: 'There is a sinister character in Chicago who is more dangerous than the nation's worst gangster. He conducts a vicious and risky business--the promotion of racial hatred, with biased whites as his steady clients. He has never engineered, as far as I know, any outrage like the Valentine Day massacre, but his atrocious activities, if permitted to continue, are sure to cause violent death to hundreds of unsuspecting American citizens who become victims of his bias plots * * * He defies all law and order in the performance of his defaming work. He is a menace to racial harmony in Chicago. This is the introduction to Joseph Beauharnais * * *.' Beauharnais, tall, loose-jointed, shifty-eyed, was dressed in a shoddy blue suit with red and white stripes, probably in answer to his 'patriotic' tendencies.'

As to damages, plaintiff averred in each Counts 1 and 2 'That by reason of the premises plaintiff has been damaged in the sum of One Million Dollars, for which he prays judgment.' As to Count 3, Plaintiff alleged 'By reason whereof the plaintiff has been damaged in his standing and reputation, and in his business and social relations, in the community in which he lives and elsewhere, in the sum of One Million Dollars, for which he prays judgment.'

The original complaint was filed by plaintiff pro se, but an amendment to the complaint showing diversity of citizenship, was signed by plaintiff and by his attorney, Lawrence M. Fine. [Same lawyer for De Rose]

Defendant's answer, among other things, averred the article declared on was published as a news item pertaining to plaintiff's activities as the founder of The White Circle League, and his actions creating and promoting racial discord and hatred. In substance, the answer alleged that the article was fair comment, and that it was written and published without malice. The answer denied that the statements therein were false and untrue and asserted that the article was published in good faith.

The trial in the District Court was before a jury. Defendant moved for a directed verdict at the close of plaintiff's evidence. The District Court granted the motion, whereupon the jury returned verdict in favor of the defendant. Judgment was entered accordingly from which this appeal was taken.

The law of Illinois is controlling. Spanel v. Pegler, 7 Cir. 160 F.2d 619, 621, 171 A.L.R. 699; Rose v. Indianapolis Newspapers, 7 Cir., 213 F.2d 227, 229. Article 2, § 4 of the Constitution of Illinois, S.H.A., provides: 'Freedom of Speech and Press-- Libel. . .

The subject matter of the Cicero riots was a matter of great public interest and concern. The press of the entire nation had given much publicity to the unfortunate occurrence. The record shows that during the violence of the Cicero riots the plaintiff was on the scene soliciting memberships for The White Circle League. Plaintiff's activities were a legitimate subject of fair criticism and comment. Criticisms directed to such a subject matter are not libelous, although severe in terms, unless they were written and published maliciously. Brewer v. Hearst Publishing Co., 7 Cir., 185 F.2d 846, 850; Kulesza v. Chicago Daily News, 311 Ill. App. 117, 35 N.E.2d 517, 521; Tiernan v. East Shore Newspapers, 1 Ill.App.2d 150, 116 N.E.2d 896, 898.

Although the criticism of the plaintiff's activities was couched in strong language, the attitude taken by the Courts where the subject matter is of great public concern may be shown by a quotation from the opinion of the Supreme Judicial Court of Massachusetts in Hartmann v. Boston Herald-Traveler Corporation, 323 Mass. 56, 80 N.E.2d 16, 19, where the court said: 'Fair comment (on a matter of public concern) may be severe and may include ridicule, sarcasm, and invective. * * * But severity and vigor in expression, whatever evidential effect they may have, are not to be confused with malice in motive. '

The question whether the words complained of are libelous per se was for the trial court to determine. Kulesza v. Chicago Daily News, 311 Ill. App. 117, 35 N.E.2d 517, 521. Construing the article according to its plain and ordinary meaning and considering the article as a whole, we are of the opinion that it did not exceed the limits of fair comment permitted in a matter of great public interest. Judgment affirmed. (http://bulk.resource.org/courts.gov, 2011)

Drawing (Edwards, L.)

On March of 1957 a settlement was reached on the damages done in the Cicero Riot for $4,300. It was not to all of the owners, but to Ms. De Rose alone.

Camille in her summation of the riot writes, "I have great respect for Negro scholars and the many Negro people of good character and principle. But there should be some method to effectively warn the Negro citizens against their politicians and so-called 'leaders.' These opportunists pretend to devote themselves in the cause of Negro 'rights.' By exaggerating discrimination and denial of 'civil rights,' they are able to whip up Negro fears, hate, and prejudice against their white neighbors. Every casual quarrel is blown up to suit the pattern." (p. 319)

In later years a website article appeared:

At Cicero, IL, police at first prevented Mr. and Mrs. Harvey Clark from moving into an apartment building occupied by whites. When a Federal court intervened, a white mob formed and reduced the interior of the building to a shambles. Of the 120 mobsters arrested, two were convicted and fined 10 dollars each.

A grand jury proceeded to indict the owner of the building, the rental agent, and the attorney of the victim. A year later, Cicero's Chief of Police and two policemen were fined from 250 to 2,000 dollars, but the fines were rescinded another year later by the U.S. Court of Appeals. Eventually, the owner of the building, Mrs. Camille De Rose, sued the Clarks and eleven other Negroes for $1,000,000, charging that they had conspired to defraud her and send her to prison and a mental institution (she was admitted to the latter). On 9/18/1951, a Cook County grand jury indicted the NAACP attorney defending the black family trying to move into Cicero, the landlady, and her rental agent, not the mob!

After the 1951 riot, Cicero whites were outraged that Gov. Adlai Stevenson had called out the National Guard, so the town flipped and voted for Ike in 1952; has been Republican ever since.

In Cicero during an MLK march, in 1966, white counter-protestors physically assaulted King.

Cicero, Illinois: racially exclusionary policies made headlines during the Civil Rights Movement and were not amended as late as 1981, still the center of controversy over non-white residents in 2000. (http://sundown.afro.illinois.edu/, 2011)

My father has kept almost everything from his life, especially the items published on the riot; although, I had to search archives to find the source of some of the papers, authors, and dates, as a lot were worn away, missing, or not included. When researching books and articles on the topic, one notices that there are many referencing the 1951 Cicero Riot as a case for race riots, segregation, and desegregation. Some had larger facts distorted and some had details off.

Camille De Rose's book was mostly a distorted version of the truth another article in the *Suburb Reader* by Becky M. Nicolaides and Andrew Wiese stated that, "The Cicero rioting started when a Mrs. De Rose, who owned the apartment house. . . Shortly after, out of spite, profit, or both, she rented an apartment to Clark." (2006) The authors mention an affidavit by Clark when in actuality the affidavit quoted is by Charles Edwards. (Edwards, 1951)

The building had more protection than the victims (Edwards, C.)

Chapter Eleven
"'I'm Still Standing,' Perspective"

Camille commented that, "Adams and Edwards are inseparable. Edwards is a silent partner in the literal sense of the word. He rarely spoke. As I said earlier, they look alike and act alike excepting that Adams talked for both. Edwards was introduced to me as the real estate agent, and, at least at the outset, they addressed each other as Mr. Adams and Mr. Edwards, unusual among office and business associates. Adams claimed that he never had any children. During the riots, the newspapers described Edwards as Adam's grand nephew-in-law! What does this contradiction signify? Whatever it signifies, it is a contradiction, and puzzling." (p. 200)

Using a person's title in their work environs, in public, or with people who are not on the same level of familiarity is out of respect and proper etiquette. When I go into a family member's office, I ask for Attorney Adams or Dr. Edwards. If out in public I address friends and family as Mr. Secretary or Mr. Mayor while later in private it would be by their name or nickname. It is even more important with Blacks in mixed company, and what my great-grandparents taught me early on.

Indictment after indictment came in. My father was vilified and indicted; he had guns put to his head and body. He was beaten, and he and all of the family were threatened, and some assaulted, and possibly one murdered. After one bad beating and threats of murder, with his well being and security disintegrating in front of him, and his life spiraling out of control, he was checked into Hines V. A. Hospital for injuries, arrhythmia, and post traumatic stress causing him to miss a court appearance resulting in a warrant being issued for his arrest.

Cars and people would suddenly appear at home and at work for both Papa and Dad. Another instance of Papa having more resources than my father was that he carried a .38 revolver and had received police and detective training. On February 23, 1942, he became a licensed "Special Officer" for the City of Tulsa. He had several guns (My favorite was the old Colt revolver with an extended barrel.) locked away in his six and one half feet, 38 inch wide, 1930 Diebold safe.

Callers would call their homes and offices saying the "N" word as well as many other expletives; they said that they would harm my mother, my aunts, my grandmother, my great-grandmother, my sister, and my brother, and many said, "We'll kill you and if not you, someone." (Edwards, 2010) On the night of July 27th four shots were fired through the window. The alarming feature of the shots and calls is that they came in at 2 or 3 o'clock in the morning, disrupting what little peace one was able to get. Obviously my parents losing the building by foreclosure turned out to be fortuitous for one moment because they had to move going from one family home to another making it more difficult for people to track them.

Shots fired at night into home. (Edwards, C.)

Death threats continued for many months on both families and their households, and increased as the trials started in late September and October. At Papa's address, 4757 South Parkway, he and Mother

Adams stayed on the second floor and her son's family, the Youngs, stayed on the first floor of the mansion while other family members stayed five blocks away in the other Adams' home, 4432 S. Michigan, which was on the same block as my parents' home and building, 921 E. 44th St. Sadly, all of these addresses were publicized in the paper.

Even Camille told of being hounded by people and chased after by cars. "Strange characters hovered around my living quarters, followed me on foot and in cars. Going out of the door was a signal to one, two, three cars to cruise around following me. I moved three times in a month." (p. 266) Moving again, she on another instance stated that several men, "Started to lunge at the door and I could see the lock giving way. I took out my pistol and knocked at the door, shouting, 'There will have to be seven, because the first six will get a bullet, so come on, I'll let you have it.' They left. " (p. 268) She pulled her gun out on other occasions as she moved three more times all near my family. She lamented that, "Meanwhile, my folks in Berwyn were receiving threats over the telephone constantly, always predicting my death. . .One car cleared me within an inch. " (p. 269) And if she was getting this treatment, you know the Coloreds who she said were behind everything forcing her to do what she did, were getting much, much worse.

Lucille Clara Young, my mother's mother, was so scared for every one especially after being assaulted and threatened. All of this exacerbated her health condition and the family moved her out of the city to my father's family home in North Chicago for safety. My sister and brother were sent to stay with family members, although they found my sister. Not only were unknown people threatening them, but as Camille's hatred against Jewell increased and growing psychological demons haunted her, she would just appear out of nowhere stalking my aunt. Then Camille moved a few blocks nearby and made the stalking on a regular basis, so it was time to move Jewell further away. Soon Jewell was sent out of the country; even missing her younger sister's wedding with less than three weeks to go.

My aunt, Jewell Young, who suffered from cerebral palsy, was at the crux of the incidents, especially in Ms. De Rose's mind, by being the owner of the building that was destroyed in the Cicero Riot which was once hers. My mother as the next oldest sister helped to raise Jewell and the rest of her siblings because of their mother suffering from heart disease and now this. My mother grew up protecting Jewell, and at this moment felt more compelled to, as the attacks and crass comments from Ms. De Rose were bantered in the media about her sister.

Going through old letters from my aunt as she traveled through England, Germany, and France told of the state of the family. Her first overseas letter that I have is from October 7, 1951, four days after the wedding. Other letters talked very briefly about the Cicero case, and about once a month was, "How is the case going?" Nothing more. I do not have the letters that were sent to her, save one after the death of Courtney Armstrong, my maternal great-grandmother, from Courtney's daughter Alice Cage Bowman.

Great-Grandmother Courtney Powell Pickett Armstrong (Mulatto) born in 1870 in Tennessee was the daughter of Alice Powell Hubbard (Mulatto), or "Miss Alu." Alice was born a slave in 1850 in Mississippi to the daughter of Rachel Powell (Black) who was born a slave in North Carolina in 1830 and the white plantation owner by the name of Jesse R. Powell born 1819 in Virginia. He also named his first legitimate child Alice, born 2 years later. Rachel was left to J. R. in his father, Cader's will of 1830; she later married Washington Powell born 1825 in North Carolina who was deeded to Cader's other son, Cader, Jr. (Hertford County, NC, Ct of Pleas, Feb Term 1831) J.R. moved from NC to MS about 1850 bringing Rachel and her mother with him. J.R.'s Tax report for 1880 shows his federal taxes at $200.34 in Canton, MS as a planter and crop as cotton for 6,678 acres.

The U. S. Census and the U. S. Freedman Bureau Records verify what our family history has been relayed from mouth to mouth and documents:

> In the 1860 Slave Schedule of the Census four are listed in one house matching our family's ages, sex, and colors to J. R. Powell as part of his 42 slaves: [Rachel's mother] Black – 70, [Rachel] Black – 32, [Alice] – Mulatto-8, and [Washington] Mulatto – 35. Once free you see Washington – 40, William - 19, Hubbard – 20, contract as Freedman laborers for R. D. Powell on August 12, 1865. In the 1870 Census you see Washington is still with J. R. as 'Farm Laborer' listed with Luis Hubbard (Black-21) who Alice later married and had Robert Hubbard with.
>
> In the 1880 Census of Canton, MS you see Alice Powell Hubbard with four kids: Della Powell – 13, Courtney Powell -10, Robert Hubbard – 7, Henry Davis – 5, living with her 'Father,' Washington -55. I am not clear whether J. R. fathered Courtney, too, or whether J. R.'s brother, William J. or the William Powell,

that is Black (deeded to Godwin, J. R's other brother in Cader Powell's will of 1830) is Courtney's father. In the 1900 Census, Canton, MS, Courtney's last name is now Pickett as 'Head' with her three (3) kids with the last name Cage: William Hernanda, Albert Azalee, and Alice, with her mother Alice Powell. In 1910 Census, Canton, Lucille Clara Armstrong shows up as 7 also with Courtney's sister Della Powell, and Courtney Armstrong as widowed. In 1920, Courtney and Lucille Clara are in New Orleans. (U. S. Census, 1860-1930 & Freedman's Bureau, 1863-1867)

In 1880, J. R.'s son, William, is back at home at 22 as a lawyer. Later he became a judge and married a Sarah Cage. Oddly enough Courtney has three (3) mixed kids by a Mr. Cage with names of William and Albert. Sallie's father who was a physician was named Albert and her brother was named Henry. Courtney told Jewell that one time Alice went to see her white half-brother W. H. who was a judge in Mississippi and he told her to never come to see him again and never to mention to anyone that they were related. She was crushed.

What we were told while growing up was that there was a terrible bus accident with Courtney and my sister while on their way to our family Thanksgiving dinner. The Chicago Transit Authority (CTA) bus was going straight for the two of them after a car turned quickly in front of it, causing the bus to veer up on the sidewalk as they were walking from one family house to another. Courtney pushed my sister out of the way of the on-coming bus and was killed. My very young sister sustained minor injuries and was in a state of shock, and her picture after the horrible accident was in the papers and captioned, "Grieves for Grandma." My great-grandfather threatened to sue and finally the City/ CTA allegedly paid $10,000 for her supposedly accidental death.

In the only letter I have to Jewell, Alice Cage Bowman called "Aunt Bit," says that no one got any money from Courtney's death, and she didn't know why anyone would say so or why they kept asking where the money was. (Bowman, 1951) It seems that there was no payment from the Transit Authority or City of Chicago; my thinking is Papa or Mother Adams said the City paid in order to calm everyone down and to make them think it was truly an accident and not murder. It worked, and only after sixty years of reading hundreds of documents and putting all of the info together in retrospect, it seems that the threats were most likely carried out. Courtney was killed and my oldest sister was almost killed.

One of Jewell's letters, this one dated October 27, 1951, reads, "Just think, today makes my first month away from home. Tomorrow I shall go to church; where I don't know, yet. Strange that I should ask about the Cicero case and then pick up an old *Times Magazine* which has something in it about the case. (The Atlantic Edition for Oct. 1, 1951)" Out of the letter's eight pages that was the only mention of the riot.

In another letter Jewell commented on an incident where her mother Lucille Clara was grabbed out in public and hurt her wrist just prior to her mother's move out of Chicago in mid October of 1951 for several months. Jewell also commented on her mother's health from the Cicero Riot's; the stress of putting on her sister's wedding on October 3, 1951; and then later her mother dealing with her mother being killed and the injury of her granddaughter on the way to the family Thanksgiving dinner on November 22, 1951. In a letter to my mother Jewell wrote, "I'm sorry mother isn't feeling well. I thought that she would get better as soon as the wedding was over. I wrote her a letter out at Helen's." (10/29/51) In a letter to her mother in North Chicago, she wrote, "In Grandma's last letter she was telling me of her concern for you... I am consoled by the fact that Grandma lived to a ripe old age without wanting for too much." (12/3/51)

On top of everything, you have to deal with the death of a loved one; an injured, traumatized child; the possibility that the people after you might have done this and might do more; and then to arrange a funeral. One of Dad's hand-written notes written while in the court room on the back of a transcript in his Cicero Riot files includes a draft for Courtney Armstrong's eulogy.

After the Thanksgiving disaster, the Christmas holidays came with family members out of the country, at school, or in hiding, and no end to the intimidation. On top of this my grandmother, Lucille Clara, who had chronic myocarditis was diagnosed with advanced breast cancer after being hospitalized for passing out from the news of the horrific accident. This caused my mother's mother to go into depression. Lucille Clara came back to Chicago and died not too long afterwards of the cancer which had metastasized with her death certificate using my parents' address; four years before the last case with the riots was settled and the mess finished.

Add some other blows and more bills; it was originally going to just be a "TKO," now it seemed like a "knock out" or "KO" was imminent.

Jewell's letters in 1951 to 1952 showed four different addresses for my mother who she wrote to weekly. It was also my father's responsibility to pay for her trip and schooling while in Europe in lieu of rent but mostly because he felt responsible for everything. This was like squeezing water out of a rock; one comment from Jewell to my mother was, "If you send me anything, please do so via cashier's checks – Charles' bank account is too elastic for my peace of mind." (Letter, 10/29/51)

Jewell in Europe for safety during riot trials (Adams, G.)

Reporters tried to publish more and more information which was putting everyone in danger. The Chicago Daily News even sent reporters and photographers to Paris, France to chase down Jewell. In a letter dated Nov. 1, 1951, she wrote, "Marcia and I went out to Citi Universitare . . .While waiting someone came up to us and asked us if we didn't mind having our pictures taken for a spread in the Chicago Daily News." Papa must have gotten to the editor because the story was never published.

After the aforementioned incidents, the threats continued and became so bad that detectives from my great-grandfather's agency were used to shadow them. Other family members in law and law enforcement called upon friends to assist to provide an around the clock watch. One was a friend of the family, Thelma Clarke, policewoman, probation officer, and committeewoman of the sixth ward, who would accompany the woman of my family when going out with her gun in a shopping bag after Courtney was killed, my sister injured, and Lucille Clara was assaulted.

Another person who came to their aid was a police sergeant named Foster who was a Kappa buddy of my uncle's just before he went to Howard Law School. The Sergeant protected the family at home in the night while off-duty. From another relative I heard, Papa's clients and former clients along with the questionable and unsavory persons of the neighborhood came to their rescue; although, some with position and money did not come to their aid. Furthermore, as relayed, no help was provided from law enforcement agencies on official duty; even the FBI investigating at the time did not offer any assistance.

The most harrowing events came when they went to testify. With all of the terrorization, and thanks to the media publishing their home and office addresses they were hounded. Dad was pulled back as the main witness, and Papa took his place against the police because he was licensed to carry a gun. It even got so bad that they agreed to try not to mention my father's name when not needed because my mother was so frightened, and of course she got her grandmother on her husband! So, Papa started saying, "His companion" when he testified against Cicero policemen and officials. One example was his testimony against Cicero Police Chief Konovsky; on the witness stand he said, "A Cicero policeman told him and a Negro companion to 'get out of town and don't come back or you'll be drilled full of holes.'. . .'The police roughed them up, threatened him and his companion, and searched his companion for a gun.' Adams testified that he had conferred with Nicholas Berkos, Cicero Village Attorney, and had been told that the citizens of Cicero had met and were, 'Ready to go into action, some with guns and baseball bats.'" My father and articles confirm that he was the "companion."

Some of the letters were threatening, some were supportive, and some were for the natural order of things. One letter to my father read, "Dear Illinois Realty Co. . . Illinois had $60,000 mortgage in my opinion that is the reason and should decide on such building. Mr. Harvey Clark should abide command. . .If colored peoples are neglected then colored peoples buy one. Do not service the war call, if at home. . .Use Democracy just for fun or for real ideas. J. Kara, Chicago." The letter did not make much sense other than you should get your own building, which is what they did.

One letter to my Great-grandfather read:

"I have some ideas which are as definite as Mr. Clark's. I would like to express them to you and ask you to explain them to Mr. Clark – in words of one syllable, so the university graduate can understand them. . .There are many white people who are disliked by white people and the disliked ones will sell or rent to colored people to get even with the white people who dislike them. The colored people should not allow themselves to be used to settle a grudge. . .I do not wish to humble the colored man. But each time he causes trouble by inciting race riots he should remember he is disturbing the race of people who freed him and his forebears. . .Working for white people gives them [colored people] salaries to help their race areas – not to move out of it. . .Please tell your Mr. Clark that he has every opportunity that the white people have – but he must exercise it among his own race – not take for himself what the white man has provided for himself. . .He [Clark] knows the cost of war – he knows better than those of us who were in the United States – but that same experience should make him voluntarily humble to the North who freed him and the South which was devastated and the people who lost so much. . .Instead he wants race war to replace the Civil War!!!? Are you encouraging him? . . .White people have the freedom to eject him. . .He should be smart enough to realize when he is offered an apt. among white people that he is being used to settle a grudge and have no part of it. Oh sure the white man may say he is the colored man's friend – but don't believe him. Mrs. Upsham, LaGrange Park"

Her stance is easy to see, but the reasoning hard to believe. I'm sure she did not know Attorney Adams was Black. He probably couldn't read her letter because it wasn't mono-syllable.

Meanwhile, my father had been attending John Marshall Law School from 1946 to 1952 during the day and was in his last semester. Because of so many subpoenas and being in jail, in meetings, or in a courthouse he was cited for falling asleep or missing classes at law school and threatened to be expelled. In addition to law school my father worked nights at the Tannery as an electrician to pay for his education, bills, and his partner's bills once he left.

My father sent a letter asking for patience and consideration because he had been in court and a "commotion." The August 10, 1951, letter to John Marshall read:

Re: Tues., July 10, Thurs., July 12, Mon., July 23, Tues., July 24, Thurs., July 25

Dear Sirs:

I have had the following absences from the summer course.

On Tuesday, July 10, and on Thursday, July 12, in my capacity as agent of the building at 6139 W. 19th Street, Cicero, Illinois, I was present during a civil commotion revolving around the property. This is a matter of public record.

On Monday, July 23, Tuesday, July 24, and Thursday, July 26, I was under treatment at the Veteran's Hospital at Hines, Illinois. I am enclosing my discharge slip from Hines hospital.

I hope that these absences can be excused. I will appreciate any consideration given.

Sincerely yours,

Charles S. Edwards (Carbon copy of original)

He was re-instated in good standing and then his grades dropped from an "A/B" student and Mensa member to "C/I" [Incomplete] in his last semester and the last phase of comprehensive exams to ready them for the bar. Of course, it is the school's responsibility to not matriculate "unsatisfactory" students.

In a letter dated October 12, 1951, Dean Noble Lee of Marshall Law School finally lets my father know that he passed last year's comprehensive exams with his reinstatement. The letter read, "I am glad to advise you that you passed the Comprehensive Examination given last August." (Original) Then on January 8, 1952, Dean Lee wrote to Dad, that he had passed the September of 1951 Comprehensive Examination.

After the incident, Dad's absences continued. His name appeared in local, national, and world wide papers and on television and radio stations hundreds of times in just the first year. Arnold Hirsch in his book, *Making the Second Ghetto*, wrote that, "The reaction to the incident [Cicero Riot] was immediate, worldwide outrage. Gov. Thomas E. Dewey of New York, visiting Singapore, was 'shocked' to find the Cicero riot front-page news in Southeast Asia; the Singapore

Straits Times even ran photographs of the mob to augment its coverage. News of the riot was also carried in the Pakistan Observer and apparently reached Africa as well." (p. 53)

Dean Lee also included in the letter stating that Dad's progress was unsatisfactory and not up to Marshall's standards. Even though Dad passed, he was threatened, like he needed additional stress. Dean Lee wrote:

> Furthermore, because experience has demonstrated a close relationship between success in the Comprehensive Examinations and success on the Bar examination, your attention is particularly called to the fact that hereafter, a failure to pass two successive Comprehensive Examinations in successive years will result in disciplinary action, regardless of whether the student's average is otherwise satisfactory and regardless of the fact that the first Comprehensive Examination failure may have been made up. (Original)

My father was told that he was again missing too many classes and the school threatened to tell the VA Loan organization that he did not deserve a loan because he was not attending school.

My father wrote the following letter in response to John Marshall on March 12, 1952:

> Dear Sirs:
>
> This will request that my absences on the following days be excused absences: Thursday, March 6, 1952; Friday, March 7, 1952; Monday, March 10, 1952; Tuesday, March 11, 1952.
>
> On the above dates I was present at the Criminal Court of Cook County as a witness in the cause of People v. Erwin Konovsky.
>
> I am enclosing a copy of the criminal subpoena.
>
> Very truly yours,
>
> Charles S. Edwards (Carbon copy of original)

Next my father received the following letter, this time form the Assistant Dean Stephen R. Curtis stating that, "By action of the Faculty, you are hereby placed on probation through the end of the semester. . . May I therefore urge you to examine your own situation fairly and honestly, including the questions of whether home or employment responsibilities are interfering with your studies so that a reduction in your schedule may be advisable; and whether you have been as diligent in your studies as you might have been." (Original)

Is it possible that the Cicero or Chicago Police or one of the Cicero town officials made the John Marshall Law School or one of its Deans a visit? Well, it took the school a while to find out that he was doing unsatisfactorily. Coincidentally this was the same time when he was to testify against the Cicero Chief of Police and his two assistants and other town officials. What saved my father more brutality this time was that Camille turned witness for the prosecution in a plea bargain clearing the Chief of malfeasance on March 22, 1952. In another simultaneous trial, the Assistant States' Attorney James A. Brown even argued for three hours for the state not to drop two (2) criminal charges of conspiracy against my father, which later failed.

The next trial started May 19, 1952, in front of Judge LaBuy in federal court on the violation of the civil rights of the "Negroes," which carried higher penalties than the first meaning, more peril. My father stated that the threats increased. Six (6) surprise witnesses testified that Cicero Officials tried to stop the riot and that our family planned the riot for personal gain and notoriety, one of whom was Broz. His concocted story helped Cicero get out of civil rights violations and Judge LaBuy's original decree before the riot to protect the "Negroes."

Another part of the problem as my father explains is that they summoned him to court making him miss class and when he got there he found out that the case was continued, and continued, and continued. He had no prior notice which would have allowed him to stay in school; his attorney Joseph Clayton was not notified either.

My father does not remember, but from reading old articles and going through his papers I counted eleven different continuances for this one case. This did not include the other several on-going cases with depositions, appeals, re-trials, and the times when the trials really were heard. Even before the riots my father's calendar showed eighteen (18) visits to the riot building showing clients and meeting with Ms. De Rose and Cicero Town and Rent Officials.

The final suit involving my father and family was settled in 1957. This was long enough to devastate his life. I wonder why he had difficulty sleeping and keeping up his grades. The correspondence from the law school continued. I guess the Dean was the good cop and the Assistant Dean the bad cop because on July 23, 1952, (a month after his expulsion) Asst. Dean Curtis wrote:

> It, consequently, becomes my disagreeable duty to inform you that by action of the Faculty you have been dismissed for

poor scholarship as of June 20, 1952, and are therefore ineligible to re-register for further study.

We sincerely hope that you will find other fields of endeavor where your efforts will produce results more satisfying to you, and if you should feel that we can give you any counsel or assistance in this regard, please do not hesitate to call upon us.

Yours very truly,
Stephen R. Curtis

To add insult to injury Assistant Dean Curtis told him that in a post script of the aforementioned letter that his "Original registration form was destroyed" and he had to re-register even though he was re-admitted and taking classes this second time for almost two years. "Consequently it would be impossible for us to issue a transcript or to verify your attendance if requested to do so by the Civil Service or any prospective employer."

Why does one arbitrarily destroy only one record? There was no water or fire damage. Even records of students that did not matriculate are kept. Why was his registration destroyed when he was ready to graduate and in the middle of comprehensive exams to ready students for the state bar?

How did the Dean, Assistant Dean, John Marshall Law School, and anyone not know what had happened when the world knew what had happened from July 10-14, 1951, in Cicero, a Chicago suburb? Dad's name, image, company were lambasted on the front page or somewhere in every paper, major and ethnic, in Chicago and suburbs for years. The trial against the Cicero Officials and Police started March 1952 and did not end until 1957 because of continuances, appeals, reversals, and new trials.

I find it hard to believe that the Dean and Assistant Dean of John Marshall Law School in Chicago did not know about the incident or the trials, as it is even harder for me to believe that cops up for major felonies in two federal cases and one state case had not asserted their influence in other parts of your life after threatening your life previously, especially if you were a Negro in 1951. Moreover, different tales were related in letters and by staff at different times.

Attorney Everett Lewy even wrote a letter in response to Dad requesting assistance, "I cannot say anything official except that you were my student and a good one. . .I am, of course, familiar with the tremendous amount of time that you devoted to business affairs while you were in school and would be glad to tell. . .Frankly, I do not know how these schools do things."

Of course the so-called accidental death of your wife's grandmother and injury to your daughter and mother-in-law, all of the visits by suspicious people, the hate letters, the threatening phone calls, and verbal assaults were done by other people who were just race haters. But wasn't that who the Cicero Mayor, Attorney, Chief, police force, and towns folk came off as being? So, logically it would seem if someone was trying to strike back, justifiably so in their eyes, through the only recourse that one had, that would put you in jail and cause your employer to pay a large judgment, wouldn't you attack, or at least attempt to maintain your status quo?

During this same trial a cloth with combustible liquid was put into his thermos while at work. Thankfully, my father had someone buy him a cup because he couldn't find his thermos right away; the culprits took too long. When he got home my mother smelled the liquid as she was getting ready to wash it and called the police. They said there was nothing they could do. (Edwards, 2011)

A couple of weeks later after his shift was over, Dad was detained at his car by Griess-Phleger Tannery security. Upon inspection they found company materials in his lunch box. The company and police arrested Dad for stealing the items but they weren't concerned that someone was trying to kill or seriously hurt him during the trial. The FBI was called in but they found nothing on either incident. However, it was enough to cause him to get fired from a superintendent who previously wrote that he was an excellent worker. The plant was nice and dropped the criminal charges. (Edwards, 2011) Who put the parts in his lunch pail? Why not instigate the concept of his not being a desirable student and getting him kicked out of school?

Was there some outside or internal influence or just some personal issue with having my father in school? When is a student with good grades who passes comp exams a bad student and poor candidate to go for the Bar? Was my father the wrong type of colored person to represent them, or just the wrong color?

Even though the Veteran's Administration paid for some of his tuition, the rest my father paid along with fees and books. This was more money down the drain, another slap. Although the NAACP rallied around the Clarks and raised several thousands of dollars for them after the incident, nothing was done to help my parents who were involved, suffered, and broke, yet still helped the Clarks and let them stay with them on more than one instance.

One article in the *Defender* stated that, "Mr. and Mrs. Harvey Clark and family were the recipients of goodwill letters from whites all over America, many enclosing checks to cover the costs of the property destroyed by hoodlums last Wednesday before the arrival of the National Guard troops, hurriedly dispatched by Gov. Stevenson. Nearly $2,000 was reported by the local NAACP branch this week in contributions, of which $1,770.65 was raised at the Monday night mass meeting." (1951, P.1) However, the NAACP's brochure titled, "No More Ciceros!" claims that, "Aug. 20 – Clark Fund increased to more than $4,000 through individuals and organizations throughout the country." (1951, P. 2)

I'm all for the National Association for the Advancement of Colored People (NAACP), and understand what the organization was working for. The $200,000 law suit filed by the NAACP on behalf of my father, my great-grandmother, the Clarks, the Scotts was led by George Leighton. Attorney White came out from Washington, DC as did Thurgood Marshall for one of the previously mentioned rallies for the Clarks. Where did the money go from the civil suit?

Dad's major legal and business fees he assumed on or before March 1, 1952, were: Atty. Edward Lewy - $4,000.00; Atty. Edward Lewy - $2,250.00; Alexander Grant Co. - $725.00; Bella Horvit - $417.48; Orvis E. Hallberg - $100.00.

During all of the riot, trials, meetings, and summons his business slipped; he was the principal in making and closing most of Illinois Realty deals as one can see on the documents and commissions he still has. Dad contributed the majority of income to the company.

The year before the riot the company saw profitable quarters. One in particular came to a total income of $4,240.32 minus expenses; their net income for said quarter was $3,285.93. Moreover, Dad's assets were double his partners, Dean Chandler, and Dad's net worth tripled Dean's because of Dean's expenditures.

Dad felt alright knowing that Dean could at least collect rent and possibly get a few deals to keep the company going, especially with Dean's mother working as a sales agent. At this point he did not oversee the company or work closely with his best friend and partner because they knew each other from growing up. Dean however took advantage of the situation and started taking liberties and mixing business funds with personal funds.

Charles' partner absconded with the company money. During one period as things were getting convoluted in Chandler's mind between business and personal expenses, Dean wrote at least seven (7) checks to himself totally $2,815.00, one to cash for $50.00. He also wrote checks for his rent and to various parties for $2,750.80, and to one particular person, Maceo T. B. for $630 and a number of checks to Leonard B. totaling $680.00. Were these gambling debts, liquor, or something else? Was Dean just a plain thief with no conscious or was he a thief pressured by outsiders to take more money and leave town? Chandler left Dad with the office bills, his coal bill, and one for his used 1950 Pontiac De L sedan. He even had the audacity of having the car insured under the company's name. So of course, Dad paid for it.

Besides checks to himself and acquaintances, Chandler did not deposit the rent that he collected from several accounts, such as the Fletcher ($589.00) and Osborne ($500.00) deposits. Two large outstanding collections which Dean absconded with were the Redels and Brinkerhoffs. Theses two accounts wanted justice, repayment, and more.

On July 1, 1952, Dad was presented with a Chattel Mortgage Foreclosure on their office from one of Dean Chandler's debtors, H. S. Redel. To make matters worse the claim was first made to Dean T. Chandler on November 20, 1951. Dean never even mentioned to my father or tried to make any attempt to settle this large claim. My parents took out a loan and set up installment payments for the Redel and Brinkerhoff obligations. They paid every debt including this one, with the Brinkerhoff debt not being paid off until the end of 1961. Not one bill his ex-partner made, did he pay from the time of the riot on.

Dean took advantage of the fact that my father was in serious trouble and pre-occupied in court on a regular basis, going to school, and working at night. Dad itemized all of their office furniture and sold it for a loss to help pay for Chandler's bills.

The last communication from my father to Mr. Chandler was a hand written note:

> I will be available anytime for a meeting with the parties you named in your letter together with you.
>
> Meetings in the past have been fruitless and filled with excuses, withheld facts, and misstatement. I can see no further need of sitting across the table with you singly.

I would appreciate in addition to the general accounting I requested a schedule of rents collected by you on apartments you were instructed to hold vacant, proceeds from our furniture sold by you, and deposits received by you, and other money.

Should you have any personal bills on the name of Illinois Realty I would appreciate you so informing the coal companies which have been writing regarding coal delivery made to 4542 Ellis Ave [Dean's home address].

I would prefer evening or Wednesday for any appointments. A letter will suffice should I not be conveniently reached by phone.

I would also appreciate a memorandum receipt for money you alleged to have paid to Mrs. Chandler and Mr. and Mrs. Williams which money constitutes the McCoo note proceeds, commission from negotiations of the McCoo mortgage, the Harris Trust Commission, and other commissions.

I would appreciate an early reply.

Cc: M/M Brinkerhoff, M/M Dyle, Mrs. Stella Chandler, M/M Williams, H. S. Redel.

Mr. Chandler did not meet with my father as requested in this note, or any other time. Dean never returned a call. He just left town without paying back any of the money he stole, and my father never pressed charges. Rumor had it that Dean was teaching at some school down in Mississippi.

Whenever, if ever life is so cruel, it is a true blessing to have faith and someone to turn to. When fired, kicked out of law school, money gone, and a new baby, he threw in the towel. Dad struggled from being defeated for awhile my mother says, and gave up on school and thoughts of starting another business.

With financial debt mounting, and Mom's support and insistence, he re-grouped and went out looking for a job. He went from job to job, and wasn't in the best mood, and started drinking "boilermakers" when he got home from trying to find a job in his trade of electricity/electronics, or the other jobs he had to take that he didn't like or met his education or aspirations. During a one year period, he was at the U. S. Post Office (2 different times), Civil Service Temporary Help with Bureau of Public Debt, and when that didn't work out he worked at a radio business, the Rosenwald Foundation, the Economy Bookstore, the Department of Public Debt, Rheem

Manufacturing, Stewart Warner Corporation, and finally the Checker Cab Co. But he stayed with it as another child was born, then me.

After applying at many places for jobs from 1952 to 1953, during a very long, cold Chicago winter, with no end to the trial in sight, he got a break when a cab slot opened up. He started driving a cab to feed his family and pay off bad debts by his ex-friend and partner. Wherever he got a fare that would end at a viable job site he would go in and apply.

Applications were filled out and he finally got a job as a worker in the Ford Motor Company as an electrician in late 1953, strangely enough at 7401 S. Cicero, Chicago. Ironically this was the street that separated Chicago from the City of Cicero. He was such a good leader that he was elected shop boss after company officials noticed that the one leading negotiations was Black and not a journeyman. He was given a break and instantly made journeyman, which also included a raise.

After stints with the Pullman Car Company and the City of Chicago, he got his B. S. in Business Administration in 1973 and his Masters in 1976 from Roosevelt University. He was motivated after my mother went back to their old alma mater and got her degree.

The aftermath of such a year liken to Job's would likely have crushed many. Such situations left many wounded with lingering effects and variant sides as the Edwards', Adams', Youngs', Scotts', Clarks', De Rose's, and others involved can attest. No one came out unscathed.

It is well documented that Camille De Rose was hospitalized for being insane, eventually was locked up, and then went into terrible bouts of depression and delusions as noted in court. She finally ended up being declared legally insane. This definitely helped with all the suits that she levied against the family.

From articles, it appears that the Clarks received approximately $4,000 from the NAACP, about $2,000 from individuals, and $1,000 from the City of Cicero for their damaged property that they still owed on. They were offered jobs in Norwalk, CT and Michelle, the oldest daughter, a new piano, which they took. I'm sure on the surface it seemed like things were going well for them, but I'm sure there was more.

In an article dated October 9th, 1962, in the *Chicago Defender* written by Ernestine Cofield, she relays the last known standing of the

Clarks prior to Harvey's death in North Carolina in 1998. The article reads:

> In their [Cicero's] persistent stand over the years, the Cicero race riots provide a dark chapter.
>
> It was a story of bloodshed, violence, and the tragic break-up of a Negro family.
>
> Several years ago there was a small item in one of the newspapers. It merely stated the Harvey Clarks were getting a divorce and it gave the grounds on which they were being sought.
>
> There was no mention in the short article of the Cicero Riot that had rocked the nation in July 1951. The Clarks were just another couple, who had decided they could live better apart.
>
> Some of the couple's friends and acquaintances felt that the Cicero riots had shaken the marriage which had lasted nine years up until those strife-thorn nights.
>
> Clark ended the interview when asked, "How did the Clarks stand up under all this. 'These things happen. . .and you find you can stand up all right. You're less than a man if you don't.'" (1962)

This clearly was the sentiment of my father, Charles Sumner Edwards, and great-grandfather, George Cornelius Adams. I remember the latter saying that, "You fight with all you got for all that's right and all that's yours." Attorney Adams re-grouped; he formed a new partnership in 1960: Adams, Montgomery, and Weston, with some of their cases being hallmarks in civil litigation.

Only history can put such events like the 1951 Cicero Riots in proper prospective and only time can heal wounds. Although to my family, we are still trying. For Chicago, the city that we grew up in and have now moved away from still harbors horrible memories that have shaded one's past and outlook.

Isabel Wilkerson wrote in her 2010 novel, *The Warmth of Other Suns*, about Chicago and Hyde Park where several generations of my family stayed:

> The neighborhood [Hyde Park] was one of the most expensive on the South Side, so blacks who moved there had to have the means just to get in. Thus Hyde Park actually became a rare island of integration despite initial hostilities. Still, it is surrounded by all black neighborhoods in a deeply divided city. Entire communities like the suburb of Cicero remained

completely off-limits to blacks, and whites would avoid so much as driving through whole sections of the south and west sides for the remainder of the century. By the time the Migration reached its conclusion, sociologists would have a name for that kind of hard-core racial division. They would call it hypersegregation, a kind of separation of the races that was so total and complete that blacks and whites rarely intersected outside of work. The top ten cities that would earn that designation after the 1980 Census. . .were, in order of severity of racial isolation from most segregated to least: (1) Chicago. (p. 398)

Sadly, the last word on the town of Cicero with its uncanny history of its residents who aren't much on civil rights is that the U. S. Housing and Urban Development (HUD) filed a law suit against Cicero landlords in 2000:

> Three owners of a suburban Chicago apartment complex were charged with housing discrimination today, after one asked prospective tenants over the telephone if they were black and then refused to rent to blacks, Housing and Urban Development Secretary Andrew Cuomo announced.
>
> Landlord Alice Calek allegedly told one caller that she could not rent to a black person because blacks didn't fit in the Chicago suburb of Cicero, where they make up about 5 percent of the population. Calek also allegedly told a caller that the last time black people moved into the area, their home was burned.
>
> In addition to charging Calek with housing discrimination, HUD filed the same charges against the other co-owners of a 24-unit apartment complex in Cicero - Camille Zatopa and Raymond Nemecek. HUD's investigation showed that three owners of the apartment complex - who are brother and sisters - have never rented to an African American in the several decades their family has owned the complex. The complex is located at 2209 61st Court in Cicero. (Sec. Cuomo, HUD Archives, April 4, 2000, HUD No. 00-70)

Fighting is a luxury, when you have resources and can stand to lose but believe you can win. If your spirit is broken and there are no more resources and your reserves consist of fumes and only faith, you retreat.

Maybe secretly it was all a welcome relief to have forgotten about such traumatic, outlandish events, especially if beaten up so, literally and figuratively. Repression and compliance can be beaten in but the ravage of the mind, heart, and spirit are so much worse. One can regress to a better time and the fact that such horrible things never happened. For many years until my probing again, the events of 1951 were never mentioned, especially the Cicero riot. The crux of the problem is a wound that formed a cistern of an unrequited will to live. When almost all that you have and know is shaken or taken except your faith.

Maybe without the events of 1951 my father would not have been such a good man and father. I would not be the person that I am, and I would not feel so loved and ingratiated to take on the task of caregiver for three very sick people in my house with the help of a sister.

It is also my opinion that he would not have the will to live that he does when countless doctors did not think he would make it out of 2009 with twenty percent heart capacity and a consuming lung disease. I believe that he is also fighting to be with my mother who suffered a massive stroke when after such a horrible start they have stayed together for 63 years, especially now that he can be strong and there for her, as she was for him in the fifties. I know that the tragedy and hardship of 1951 has bolstered his mind, heart, and spirit. He is re-paying a debt: a love and strength that got him through his "worst moment."

However, to one family, especially my father, the rippled hatred and bias of one incident spread into every aspect of our family's life and the cataclysmic spiral of bad luck in such a time in such a city continued to suck my father under in an eddy of failures. Family thankfully came to the rescue. To God and his testament my father navigated treacherous waters, and when needed our family and a good Samaritan threw him a rope.

One can see from a letter dated September 26, 1972, to Roosevelt University to accept him as a student how the incidents of 1951 still gnawed at him. My father wrote:

> In October of 1945, I returned to the plant [Greiss-Pfleger] where I was previously employed and served as president of the C. I. O. Local whose membership majority was foreign born. Both parents passed away within a year. I enrolled in John Marshall Law School, passed examinations for Real Estate Broker and General Insurance Broker and with limited financing started a business. Business was good, expansion was

rapid, and I made the financial pages with several successful ventures.

Being overextended, the firm went under with great subsequent profits to persons [great-grandparents and Williams] who had advanced the short-term financing. After the firm went under I discovered my partner had collected approximately $5,000 dollars from clients and dropped out of contact. I returned to the trade and paid off these funds without contribution or recovery from the partner. I worked seven days a week for three and a half years for the Ford Motor Company in plant wide electronic maintenance. By this time, the John Marshall Law School records, showed, 'not allowed to continue for failure to take comprehensive examinations ... Dropped out after not being allowed to continue.'

I worked twelve years on a rotating shift as a Repairer of Circuits for the City of Chicago, I have taught Electronics part-time for six years and full-time for two years for the Public School System. I have worked as a lineman for contractors for four years, taught electronics as a civilian instructor for the Navy and, between jobs I have worked under five local unions.

I have currently been awarded and have been attending summer school under the International Brotherhood of Electrical Workers Founders Scholarship for journeyman electricians and, while my card is active under Local 9, I am currently working as an electronics instructor at Dunbar Vocational High School as a temporary under a trade certificate.

Three of my seven children are in colleges this semester.

I am fifty-one years of age this date. I am still pursuing the achievement I feel I am capable of attaining. I have 882 hours of law courses, many certificate courses (trade oriented), and 134 ½ hours submitted to Roosevelt.

My objective is to find that certain corporation which could use a person of my adaptability, education, minority and experience to advantage.

Respectfully, Charles S. Edwards

I now see why my family never mentioned the Cicero Riots. More importantly I understand why my parents never did, and why sixty years later my father still pauses, regresses, and speaks in a dull ache of a voice. What few words come out are short with bitter taste, and elicit pain then a tear. I am glad now in retrospect that some family member changed the subject, put me in my place, or kicked my shin.

There are many second takes of my father on a tape recorder trying to talk about the Cicero Riots because I asked. It is worse on the video recorder. After practice, breaks, and talking, we can get ten minute clips on a video recorder, then he can't go on or drifts off; we stop and do something else, then start again another day.

My mother with her positive attitude kept him going; she embodies the principle and adage constantly drummed into us from Mother Adams that, "Thoughts are things." She would cut out sayings and post them, and include notes in his lunch box. She would share those with us whenever we had difficult moments, because of race or just life, such as:

A lesson in 'heart' is my little ten year old daughter, who was born with a muscle missing in her left foot and wears a brace all of the time. She came home one beautiful spring day to tell me that she competed in 'field day' – that's where they have lots of races and other competitive events.

Because of her leg support, my mind raced as I tried to think of encouragement for her; things I could say to her about not letting this get her down – but before I could get a word out, she said, 'Daddy, I won two races!' I couldn't believe it! And then she said, 'I had an advantage.'

Ah, I knew it. I thought she must have been given a head start. . .some kind of physical advantage. But again before I could say anything, she said, 'Daddy I didn't get a head start. . . My advantage was I had to try harder.' (unk.)

In defense of my great-grandfather - I know he thought of my father as the son he never had and loved him very much. It's just that he was trying to save himself and became myopic in that endeavor. His law firm suffered and many clients who had believed him white now dropped him once Camille went through her rants and tirades in public and the media. She even commented, "After the first incident Adams did not appear to have many clients nor much legal work." (p. 159)

And thus, a great family, relationship, and business arrangement "bit the dust" as each man tried to save his own self from drowning. It's just that as my father and I believe, Papa had more resources and reserves. He had only one to think of and she was a force to reckon with on her own, and he had many.

The intelligent, reserved gentleman had suffered inwardly, but you would hardly know unless he had one too many "Jacks," before he stopped drinking. He picked himself up with the help he got, from God and family, and recovered. His advantage was he worked much harder, and used his "adaptability, education, minority, and experience to advantage." It's just a shame that he suffered so dearly. You might get an inkling of the chasm if you knew and lived with him about how much the Cicero Riot incident scared, mortified, and distorted his well-being, stability, and security, as well as the family's and the extended family's. My mother and father, after sixty three years of marriage, still cite the Cicero Riot as their defining moment, and my father cites it as his nadir. (Edwards, 2011)

Growing up we could never quite pinpoint what had left such deep wounds. Of course a child's perception of a parent, or adult, is always different than one of another adult or to the public. As a middle-aged adult I am even more impressed by his resilience that he did not go the route of Camille, or they the Clarks.

Loewen avers to the fact of the hurt felt by my father and other Blacks:

> No other group, not even Native Americans, has been so disparaged by the very structure of American society. No other group has been labeled a pariah people – literally to be kept outside...
>
> Successful African Americans may be particularly upset by these slights, because their peers, elite whites, are the least likely of all white Americans to accept African Americans into their neighborhoods and associations. As Ellis Cose famously raged, 'I have done everything I was supposed to do. I have stayed out of trouble with the law, gone to the right schools, and worked myself nearly to death. What more do they want? Why in God's name won't they accept me as a full human being?'
>
> It is frustrating: even voicing the hurt can hurt...
>
> After experiencing some of Chicago's sundown neighborhoods and sundown suburbs firsthand in 1965, Martin Luther King, Jr. observed, 'Segregation has wreaked havoc with the Negro...Only a Negro can understand the social leprosy that segregation inflicts upon him. Every confrontation with restriction is another emotional battle in a never-ending war.' (p. 349-350)

We guessed that Dad was disappointed he had to leave law school and set aside his dreams to make enough money to take care of his large family, because as a family of nine we knew hand me downs and economizing. In the sixties, they recovered somewhat with the help of Green Stamps, Bowman bottle tops for Riverview, scavenger hunts for money in Lincoln Park, betting on horses, taking Wonder Bread to go fishing with, etc. These were a way of life.

We were middle class in our own house only by their labored efforts. If they did not work as hard, we would have been a family struggling from one paycheck to the next to make ends meet. My mother worked, and at times my father worked three jobs at a time. We never understood how the family had money and we didn't. As a child you were afraid to ask. As I got older I did but got rebuked.

We knew Dad's father was one of the founding fathers of a small town, spoke fluent Polish, and that he worked in the Steel Mill as a fireman, (The one who stoked the fire, not the one who put it out.), and his mother stayed at home because of a failing heart which she died early from, and we have inherited in some form, i. e. heart disease, arrhythmia, and mitral valve prolapse.

Both parents were listed at one point as half white and half slave. In the 1900 Census the mother was listed as white and the father was listed as black. In a small town the family had a large tract of land, which we were told was theirs because of his mother's family who was white and left it to them. My father, his parents, Charles I and Katie Lou, and two siblings stayed at one end and their grandparents to them, James and Mattie Thompson stayed at the other end.

Only until this project did my father and the family find out that James and Mattie were not their grandparents. It turns out that Mattie is Katie's maternal aunt. After much time in libraries and searching archives, I found out their maiden name was Harrison. My father never knew his true mother's maiden name nor met his maternal grandparents because he was never told their name, and he has no idea who his paternal grandparents are except that probably the name was Charles or Robert. The only other clue was that of a paternal half-brother, William Harold Patterson.

William was a First Sergeant in the Philippine Insurrection and later World War I. He was murdered while asleep in his barracks in the Philippines. After several attempts to get records from the U. S. Government, each saying they had no record; we finally got a response that his records were burned in the fire of July 1973. I missed that newsflash. So, I sent them info from my research in the archives as requested so they could re-create their records.

My father's older sister, who is the oldest remaining member on both sides of the family, at 94, who lives with me doesn't even know my name. It's too bad I did not start this project before Alzheimer's set in. One document shows that her mother's maiden name besides Harrison, then Thompson, was really Schweigert. (Cook Co., 1911)

In the Master Thesis of James Dorsey, he states, "Blacks came to Lake County during the Reconstruction Period. However, Blacks did not settle in North Chicago until approximately 1889. . .Blacks to settle here (in approximately 1905) were L. C. Evans (Charles' in-law), Fannie Harrison Evans (Charles' aunt), Charles Edwards (Charles' father), and O. W. Evans (Charles' nephew). There were several other families who were considered as early pioneers. They were the Barretts, the Bobos, the Montgomerys, and the Thompsons [James & Margaret]."

Jim and Mattie had adopted Mattie's sister, Versie's child, Catherine Schweigert, as found out from Katie Lou's marriage license in 1911 at the age of fifteen. After searching through family papers and finding snippets of info, I find that the white man that did not marry my great-grandmother was named William. In checking Census records, I find a William Schweigert, first a jeweler then bank president, lived in Augusta, GA, twenty-six miles from my great-grandmother. He was born July 1855 in NY and his parents John and Rosanna were immigrants from Wurtenberg, Germany.

I thought that this must not be the right William Schweigert because he was a descendant of a German immigrant. Upon further inspection, it seems that this is the only William Schweigert in the region, and that on three Census reports he had three different young Black girls living with him as a servant. The 1890 Census which doesn't exist anymore would be where my great-grandmother, Versie, might have been. In 1895, she gave birth to Catherine Schweigert, and one year later William had another "Catherine Schweigert" with his legal wife. In 1900, Versie was living with another man, Taylor Garner, as a servant. In 1910, she is shown as his wife. (U. S. Census, various years)

The census of 1900 showed Catherine Harrison as a niece at six and race as "Mulatto," and the 1910 census had the Thompsons and Katie Lou as "White." (U. S. Census) "The Thompsons had no children and as was the custom of that day, families would allow one of their children to be adopted by another family member." (Edwards,

2011) My parents even discussed giving me away to my father's sister who I was named after and her husband Archie. I did find Versie's mother's family the Harrisons in Edgefield, South Carolina; her parents were Andrew (1830) and Carey Ann (1840), and Andrew's mother was Margaret Harrison born in 1800.

Charles Sumner Edwards I, my grandfather, knew the Thompsons from South Carolina where he was born in Greenwood in 1880. He came up North to Lake County after Jim Thompson, who he worked with in SC, because Jim said he found him a job. Charles stayed with them and later married their daughter/niece. He had a stroke on October 8, 1939, and my father started his first job at 14 on October 20, 1939.

The Lake County, Illinois, *News-Sun*, wrote about an aunt, Fannie Evans and her husband with my grandfather as the founders of the first Baptist Church in North Chicago. (unk.). The Thompsons owned most of the land in one area that was two blocks west of Lake Michigan at 14th and Lincoln and the Edwards a small portion at the southern end. The Evans were on the west side of this large tract of land. On the fourth corner of the land of the three family members, they founded the First Baptist Church (First A. M. E. Church) in 1905. The new building in 1921 has "J. S. Thompson, L. Evans, & Chas. S. Edwards," as three of the four on the cornerstone.

My father's family (Charles, Catherine, James, Margaret, Fannie, and William) is buried in Oakwood Cemetery in Waukegan. Strangely enough my mother's family is buried in Oakwood Cemetery in Chicago.

We each have different skin tones and look differently even if we have the same parents; just as Minerva found out through her séances that Mary and Mollie were her older sisters born to the same parents. Both were Frank's children; there is no sure formula when combining DNA.

Of the stories told to me as a youngster, the one about her father running away from the plantation and Mollie and Mary is true. Frank Lampton joined the Union Colored Troops of the 16th Infantry, Company H to fight in the Civil War after the incident. Being Mullato and able to read and write, they made him a Sergeant when he enlisted in Clarksville, Tennessee, a border town of Hopkinsville, KY in 1862. After being demoted to Private when the war ended as he was leaving service so as not to pay him the higher pension, he re-joined Lucinda Campbell Lampton, and was finally able to marry her on April 18,

1866. (Tennessee Archives, 1866) They had four more children, one being my maternal great-grandmother Minerva named after his sister. He also inherited the 1,000 acres that he was a slave on. The men of his family farmed the land and the women ran a washing and cleaning business until Mother Adams moved to Chicago in the 1880's; later she brought them up in the 1890's.

    The name "Johnson" is just the common name my great-grandmother used for a slave owner. After many months of research, I found the property ledger of them next to the cattle and horses, and later a Freedman's Bank Account. Frank's father's real name is Ambrose Morrison, and my great-great-great grandmother was Delilah Lampton. Frank sold the property and split the proceeds with his siblings Albert, Howard, Minerva, and Mary Jane. Frank moved with Albert to Chicago where Lucinda and her mother Susan opened up their own laundry business following Minerva with her $100 stake to go to school. Lucinda's mother "Sucky" was a Creek Native American; she was born 1807 in Kentucky and died at the age of 84 and fathered Lucinda out of wedlock with a Randall Bradshaw, who was White, according to her death certificate. Lucinda died in 1915 at 73 being survived only by the two daughters in Chicago and her husband Frank who died in 1923 at 100 years and almost three months. Frank is just barely darker than Lucinda who looks red and their daughter a combination of the two, although some of this can be attributed to photography. There are so many shades of the same color; just as we live in a society where there probably isn't any true un-mixed race.

    Growing up I knew only a few of the older generation, my great-grandparents, George and Minerva, her son, and four great aunts. One great aunt stayed on the first floor of one of the houses my parents owned, 6810 S. Dante. My fond memories of her were going to the store daily to buy tobacco in a bag and beer for her. I learned to roll a cigarette and wash my hair with beer from her. I also remember many a time taking care of and cooking for my siblings, as aunts and uncles also helped out. Every Saturday my father tried to not work in the evenings and he would make us chili. It was very good because all of the cousins were there. Or maybe it was the folks' turn to reciprocate the kid sitting.

    As a matter of fact by the day of the week you could tell what we were having for dinner: Mondays – meatloaf, Tuesdays – spaghetti, Wednesdays – baked chicken, Thursdays - chicken and dumplings, (made from biscuits), Fridays – fish sticks, or fish, if we caught any.

For lunch it was bologna or if we were lucky salami. To this day I refuse to eat bologna. And of course on Fridays, I was glad we were Catholic because it meant tuna fish. On Sunday morning we all marched off to Catholic Church taking up the whole pew. Then, off to the great-grandparents until they died for the same brunch every week.

There are always good people to off set the bad ones. Eventually Dad got his real estate broker's license back and became a multi-million dollar seller. He taught many a good student in and out of high schools; he taught our Navy and thirteen princes of the Royal Saudi Navy; and he climbed poles in the middle of the night during blizzards and the fierce winds and temperatures of Chicago.

Charles Edwards blazed inroads as the first black union electrician in 1941 in the Chicago area and first Black lineman, and has been with the International Brotherhood of Electrical Workers (I. B. E. W.), Local 9 since 1953 as a member.

Charles Sumner Edwards II, 1951 (Unk.)

His autobiography continues:

I was employed by several contractors as a journeyman lineman. I also worked for the City of Chicago as an 'Electrical Repairer of Circuits.' With the electrical experience, technical courses, and university education I taught electricity and electronics in high schools, colleges, the U. S. Navy, and the Royal Saudi Navy.

To make a move into education, I was helped by the I.B.E.W. Founder's Scholarship Award. This honor was an achievement due to my being a member of a trade union. This scholarship made possible my finishing up my degree at Roosevelt University which I started from 1947 to 1948.

It was the winter semester of that year at Roosevelt where I first met my wife. A friend from class set me up on a blind date with Anna Langford to accompany him on his blind date with my future wife. They were both smart and beautiful, but [Mom] and I just hit it off and talked the whole night away. The next night I was over her house for dinner and months later we were married.

With the earnings received from working as a member of building trade unions and my wonderful wife, we supported and were able to give each of our seven children a college education.

I have been fortunate to be able to use my skills for volunteer work in several communities where we lived. (1983)

Everywhere, in almost every city that I have traveled with him, he has met a former student, of all colors, backgrounds, and income. Each greets him with a smile and a firm handshake and thanks him for the difference that he made in their lives. "Mr. Edwards if not for you I would be locked up or dead." (Lawyer-Chicago) "Mr. Edwards you helped me get into the union and I was able to take care of my sick mother." (Electrician-Dowagic) If you needed help, he helped; ask the Clarks.

He now battles a consuming disease but you wouldn't know it. As I leave him on his antibiotic transfusion or nebulizer too long, he's not irritated, nor does he shout or complain. I apologize and there's that smile and graciousness.

I started this novel or journey in my teen years then worked on it again some thirty years later as fiction. Only since my father got very ill and I had to take over all of his affairs and I came across the Cicero documents; now having permission, I started putting more and more together and decided to make the novel non-fiction. When he got better he gave me permission to go through all of his papers and Papa's papers that he kept locked away. Also, I think as he has gotten sicker he wants to tell his side of the story, so that we will know and have a lesson learned; "Enjoy the good and learn from the bad," my Mom would say. Now I know they have lived this expression.

As all things heal with time; this one has not. Only the memory saves the agony. Just as current writers relate the tale of the 1951 Cicero Riots and their subsequent impact to history and current times, you can also see how information has changed, giving me another reason to write this tale. Different sources like Camille or the City of Cicero painted facts their own way, and others recount it liken to the children's game of "Telephone." The *International Socialist Review* states that, "Readers can glean fascinating details of desegregation struggles in housing and education, such as the 1951 white riot in Cicero, Illinois, in response to a Black family renting an apartment." (ISR Issue 71, May–June 2010)

Sugrue in his book, *Sweet Land of Liberty*, writes, "In Cicero, Illinois, just west of Chicago, a riot broke out in 1951 when thousands of angry whites attacked an apartment complex as a black family attempted to move in. Adding insult to injury, a grand jury indicted the black family and the white agent who had rented the apartment to them on charges of 'conspiracy' to lower property values. Their efforts were successful in keeping Cicero all white for decades. . .In 1980, one tenth of one percent of Cicero residents were black, the vast majority of whom lived part of the year in cinder-block dormitories at a horse racing track were they worked. (2008, p. 228) Obviously Mr. Sugrue had the color of the agent wrong; my father, who was the agent, is Black.

And so, we look at this journey, as in anyone's life. Every choice you make shapes your destiny. Some may be bitter and curse fate or turn from God. Still others embrace providence, wrestle with it, and put it either behind them or over them. Just as one of my mother's favorite expressions, "Pick yourself up, dust yourself off, and start all over again," (Kerns & Fields, 1936) comes from one of my favorite movies, *Swing Time*, with Fred Astaire and Ginger Rogers.

My parents raised us to believe in Proverbs 3:

My child never forget the things that I have taught you. Store my commands in your heart. If you do this you will live many years, and your life will be satisfying.

Never let loyalty and kindness leave you! Tie them around your neck as a reminder. Write them deep within your heart.

Then you will find favor with both God and people, and you will earn a good reputation.

Trust in the Lord with all your heart.

Do not depend on your own understanding.

Seek his will all you do, and he will show you which path to take. Don't be impressed with your own wisdom. . . .

My child don't reject the Lord's discipline, and don't be upset when he corrects you.

For the Lord corrects those he love, just as a father corrects a child with whom he delights.

Joyful is the person who finds wisdom, the one who gains understanding. For wisdom is more profitable than silver, and her wages are better than gold. . . .

Don't withhold good from those who deserve it when it's in your power to help them.

If you can help your neighbor now, don't say, 'Come back tomorrow, and then I'll help you.'

The Lord curses the house of the wicked, but blesses the home of the upright.

The Lord mocks the mockers but is gracious to the humble.

The wise inherit honor, but fools are put to shame. (Holy Bible, New Living Translation)

Papa, George C. Adams, died on April 1, 1971, in Chicago. Other than my father he was the only adult male in my life in my formative years. It was not until I became an adult that I was told that George C. Adams was not my biological great-grandfather. He should have been; I knew and loved him like he was, and he looked like me and almost everyone else in the family.

Atty. George C. Adams outside his law office in downtown Chicago, 1951 (Unk.)

I then decided to research my real great-grandfather, Samuel E. Young, the one who I thought early on was a great uncle, and "Policy Sam." Just recently I acquired Sam E.'s death certificate which states that he died at 1 am in the rear of 547 W. Monroe or 5472 Monroe. Unfortunately the coroner's writing is not clear, and no written documentation or definite memory exists of his death. The former address would add some legitimacy to the tale I knew when I was younger because Clinton Street and Monroe Street were right across the street from the C&NW railroad station. Samuel being out mysteriously, was kidnapped, drugged, and the excitement with his kidney problems caused his dying.

Now going through family documents and listening to family stories for this novel, there might be a slight chance that our Sam was the original "Policy Sam." There are tales of many people coming in and out of one of the family houses. One recount was each morning someone brought in sawdust and a policy wheel into the basement. More than one peeked in and saw large amounts of money on tables. On the first floor was the bookie area behind the séance area.

The family was threatened during the Prohibition era in the early 1920's by the white mafia and gangsters to stop their policy and bookie joint by one of Capone's people. Rumor has it that later Papa visited Capone at his house on 7300 S. Prairie to settle matters. The family slowed down at first, but eventually got out of the gambling business completely after the 21st Amendment in 1933.

However, if the latter home address, 5472 Monroe, is correct for Sam Young, which you hope that a relative is doing the right thing, then it could mean that Sam was near his home when he died. After much research, I found that there was not only the east-west Monroe Street that still exists but that in 1900 there was also a north-south Monroe Avenue, which is now Kenwood Ave., where my great-grandmother moved to before she died. The census shows this would have been the 7th Ward in Chicago's Hyde Park, North Township, Roll T624-247, Bounded by: E. 55th St., S. Kimbark Ave., E. 56th St., S. Monroe Ave. (Kenwood), E. 57th St., S. Woodlawn Ave. According to records the City of Chicago changed the street names and distances from State and Madison just after this.

In a "Look at Cook," website, they provide info to interpret Chicago's 1900 & 1910 Census pages, wards, and enumeration districts before and after the street changes in 1909:

    1. In 1900, street addresses were not based on the Chicago Grid System. There was no way to determine how far any 1900 address was from the base lines of State St. and Madison St. When researching addresses for a census before 1909, the pre-1909 address must be converted to the new numbering system. For example: An address obtained from a 1900 death certificate was 602 W. 39th St. This address was at the corner of 39th Street and Wentworth Ave. In 1930, this same address was changed under the 1909 new numbering system to 200 W. 39th St.

    2. In 1900, each street was assigned an address independent of the streets parallel to it. Do not assume that an address on one street would be in a parallel location on the street that is right next to it. For example: 400 S. Wentworth Ave. would not necessarily be parallel to the 400 S. Princeton Ave. address, which is the street right next to it.

    3. Before 1909, even and odd numbered addresses were not assigned to a specific side of a street. In 1900, Odd and Even numbered addresses were assigned on BOTH sides of the street. For example: Before 1909, The address of 603 W. 39th St. could be right next door to 604 W. 39th St. and they could both be on the same side of the street. After 1909, even numbered addresses were assigned to the north and west sides of streets and odd numbered addresses were assigned to the south and east sides . . .

4. In 1909, in addition to street NUMBER changes, street NAME changes were also assigned. After identifying your target ED in the 1900 Census, remember that post 1909 street addresses may be completely different than the street addresses you find in the Census Enumeration District you have selected. The 1900 Census will list the addresses and street names in existence in 1900.

5. Directional Coordinates did not exist for the 1900 census, but were included on the maps to help you locate addresses on current day Chicago Street maps. (http://alookatcook.com, 2011)

Oddly enough if the second interpretation of address is correct, with all of the noted changes, the house where Minerva died was on the exact same street almost in the same location where Sam died some seventy years earlier. Besides what was mentioned previously, the larger numbers on streets were dropped on blocks; 5472 and 5491, two street numbers of family members were changed to lower numbers. Mother Adams did say she would never re-marry until her son Siegel, named after the store where Sam worked, was grown. She kept her word.

Still there is no reason why Samuel was out this late, but maybe he went out for a couple of drinks, which would cause or exacerbate his kidney disease. The coroner did put down Bright's Disease as contributing to death; this is uncommon for someone of thirty and being able to work on his feet all day as a porter, and no one to have noticed the outward signs of the disease. So, possibly his death was helped.

According to "Doctor's Treatment" website:

Under this name [Bright's Disease] we understand a chronic inflammation of the kidney. . .The first one results oftentimes as a sequel of the acute form of Bright's disease; the second seems to occur from habitual excesses in eating and drinking. . .

Symptoms - In whatever way the disease begins, a certain group of symptoms manifest themselves after the lapse of a few months. First among these is dropsy. This begins, as has been stated, in the feet, and gradually proceeds up the limbs, until finally the entire body becomes swollen, sometimes to an enormous extent. . .After a time the body and limbs become so unmanageable from the dropsical swelling that the patient is unable to walk. By this time there are usually some sores on the legs, and the skin is the seat of intolerable itching. . .The appetite becomes impaired, there is some indigestion and even dyspepsia; in many cases there is a constant tendency to diarrhea and the formation of gas in the intestine. Later in the disease vomiting often occurs in a peculiar violent and sudden way, which has led to the employment of the term 'explosive vomiting.' The breathing, too, is impaired sooner or later in this disease; sometimes by the accumulation of watery fluid-that is dropsy-in the cavity of the chest. This is especially apt to be the case if, as often occurs, there is also disease of the heart.

Among the symptoms, too, are some which must be referred to the nervous system. Among these is obstinate and frequently recurring headache, attacks of dizziness, impairment of sight, and neuralgia in different parts of the body. As the affection approaches a fatal termination, occasional transient delirium is not infrequently observed; and for some days before death the patient frequently lies in a state of stupor, interrupted perhaps by occasional convulsions. . .Treatment - In the vast majority of cases the disease is not recognized until it is too late to expect recovery under any plan of treatment;. . .Among the most important of these is the observance of proper sanitary regulations. The patient should carefully avoid exposure to wet and cold; should not undergo physical or mental fatigue; should avoid excesses at the table or otherwise. (http://www.doctortreatments.com/Chronic-Brights-Disease.html, 2011)

After Papa died, Mother Adams' dementia got worse. I had moved down to live with her and my aunt Jewell in Hyde Park on a permanent basis that summer when I turned pro in tennis and went off to college. This turned out to be the last summer. There were many chains and locks, four on the front door alone. Still they could not keep Minerva from wandering; she .was "Going home."[God, heaven and family] Much worse as the sun set she did not know my aunt or me and she did not want to be around you because she was frightened. The oddest thing, though, the only one she remembered was "Sister." "Sister" was the nickname given to my mother, and her phone number was sewn into Minerva's coat along with a card in her purse. Each time that she escaped she was trying to find "Sister" to take her

"Home." Still they could not keep Minerva from wandering; she was trying to "Go home" and find "Sister."

The last memorable incident of one of her escapes was when she was rescued by the police after she got on a bus and stayed on it until she got to an all-white area probably trying to get to Hawthorne Racetrack; the driver called her in because he was at the end of his line at the border of Cicero. At the police station she told them to call Sister and she would drive her home. My father answered the phone and the police asked for her sister, and candidly one officer asked if her sister would be able to drive at her age.

Shortly afterwards Minerva broke her hip and died in the summer of 1972. George and Minerva are buried next to each other along with my grandmother Lucille, my great, great-grandparents, Frank & Lucinda, my true great-grandfather, Samuel, and my aunt Jewell in the family plot in Oakwood Cemetery near the Confederate Mound where approximately 6,000 Confederate soldiers are buried. Oddly after all the troubles they had from racial prejudice that their final resting place is here; or maybe God sent a message instead of Snowball that we are all the same to Him.

After this year I started spending summers with my aunt and uncle in D. C. Summers were a lot more fun with a doctor and a Federal Employee who traveled the world and took me with them as their babysitter. Alas, the "Bears' Summer Vacation" is another story.

My great-grandmother spelled no at times with an "e." In my younger days, not understanding, I thought she couldn't spell. However, one day she explained it to me; it meant no with emphasis, no exceptions, "N-O-E, no! And I do mean No!"

The Cicero Riots of 1951 went down in the records as the second worst race riot in Chicago history. Until this time my father and great-grandfather were blamed for trying to integrate an unwilling town for personal gain and notoriety; neither was true. I would doubt that anything physically happened between Camille and my great-grandfather because Papa was religious and never drank. As far as the property issue, I don't know because I never talked to him or read anything he wrote on that topic other than in trial transcripts.

My father and I have talked and I've read all of his papers. He, along with the rest of the family, was merely trying to make a living. He advertised to rent an apartment; the Clarks answered the ad. If they had not in some minds the riot would still have happened. I hope I have dispelled those notions. Nevertheless, if you wish to accept this inane concept as many have gone to their graves believing, then so be it. Blame it on the times, our country, "Jim Crow," Cicero, but not them. Thankfully, one thing is for sure; race relations are much better sixty years later. Look at President Barack Obama coming from the same Hyde Park in Chicago.

I get lost in trying to trace the many ethnicities of my family lost to the times, slavery, and the long forgotten white forefathers (Mr. Adams, Mr. Stious, Mr. Powell, Mr. Armstrong, Mr. Schweigert, Mr. Bradshaw, Mr. Morrison, and Andrew) some without a first or last name. I am happy with whom I am and how I look, but when I think of how my history unfolded, I am rueful of what was endured, as well as amazed. Now that I have finally gotten some hold on most of the members of the family tree, my pedigree comes out to 7/16 Black, 1/16 Native American, and 8/16 White. Just as in the fifties, though, even for my great-grandfather who was 12.5% Black, only the color is seen.

Camille's closing statements in her book, *The Cicero Riot Story*, are as follows: "Isn't it true that there is no biological discrimination? Do you know that by far the greater majority of Negroes are of mixed ancestry? All of us of the white race are immigrants who fled oppression from the lands of our origin. We have taken this land from the Indians whom we have routed and mistreated. We can not pretend to have our pages of history lily white." (p. 315) "We dislike the unlike…Time will take care of our unlikeness, as time is showing signs of development of an American type, where the white are becoming browner and the dark are becoming lighter." (p. 320)

Here were two Black men, George C. Adams and Charles S. Edwards II, falsely accused, and even though they were told "No" they found a way, even before Civil Rights. And, our family provided a welcome supporting cast then, and continues the struggle now.

Today, if you meet my father or spend any time with him you will know his mettle. From the highest statured to the least, from high politicians to doctors and caregivers, or some one in a shelter he volunteered at, each mentions what a nice, intelligent guy he is and how pleasant he is to talk to. He is a yes without exception.

The family looked at the incidents of 1951 as horrifically bad luck; "It's all how you look at it." (Edwards, 1964) They kept their faith and stuck together. I see why they chose to take the high road on what happened. Who wants to believe that someone in your family was murdered; people injured; lives destroyed over a mere property which led to Chicago's second worst race riot in history only because they were African-American? They have fought the good fight; they have finished the race; they have kept the faith. (*Holy Bible*, 2 Timothy 4:7-8)

As I finish this novel I recall a reading from *Our Daily Bread* written by Dennis J. Hahn, titled, "Trouble:"

Does it surprise you that trouble is a part of life? Probably not. We all know trouble close-up and personal—bad health, empty bank account, blighted love, grief, loss of job, and the list goes on. . . but trouble whether it is common to man or unique to Christians, can reveal to us the moral fiber of the soul. . .

I have never seen a golf course without hazards. They are part of the game. Golfers speak of the courses with the most hazards as the most challenging, and they will travel a long way to test their skill against the most demanding 18 holes. . .

Let's not think it strange when trouble comes, for God is using it to test the stamina of our souls. The best way to handle trouble is to commit our 'souls to Him in doing good, as to a faithful Creator.' (p. 19) 'Great triumphs are born out of great troubles.' (2011)

Addendum

Vitae George Cornelius Adams

(Unk.)

Born:
February 3, 1889 in Rayville, LA
to Charles J. and Violet (nee Gibson) Adams

Married:
December 7, 1921 to Minerva, nee Lampton, Young

Died:
April 1, 1971 in Chicago, IL

Education:
Muskogee Manual Training High School, 1914
L. L. B. Howard University Law School, Washington, DC, 1917

Experience:
Lawyer, 1917 – 1971
Clerk, U. S. Army Quartermaster's Dep't.
Secretary, National Grand Charity Dep't. Masons 1930
Grand Attorney – Masons, State of Illinois 1925
Candidate for Alderman, 1923
Candidate for Illinois Legislature, 1924-26
Special Officer #158-A, City of Tulsa (2/23/42)
Ordained Minister in 1960, Invisible Science Church
Publisher/Editor *Chicago World and The Enterprise*
Columnist for the *Chicago Defender*, "Legal Advice"
Columnist for the *Chicago Whip*, "Legal Hints"

Awards:
Presidential Certificates of Appreciation -
  Signed by Pres. Roosevelt & L. B. Hershey: 4 yrs., 2 yrs., 1 Yr.
  Signed by Pres. Eisenhower in Wash., DC on March 31st 1957
  Signed by Richard Nixon
Selective Service System in administration of the Military Selective Service Act of 1967, Awarded June 30, 1971
The Selective Service medal - Congressional Certificate of Merit, Signed by Harry S. Truman & Lewis B. Hershey
Presidential Appointment as Government Appeal Agent – 1965 by Lyndon B. Johnson Local Board #4 – Chicago, IL
Bar of the Supreme Court, 1922 – Cornelius J. Jones

Famous Cases/Clients:
Garret Morgan – Patent for Red Light
Muskogee Creek National Tribe
Jesse Binga
Ed Jones
Robert Abbott

Organizations:
National Bar Association, One of Founders in 1925
Chicago Bar Association
Grand Masons
Tau Delta Sigma
Urban League
YMCA
The Idlewilders
The "Old Tymers" Club,
Howard University Chicago Alumni
The Oklahoma Club

Business Pursuits:
Adams Secret Service Agency
Adams Detective Agency/ Burns & Lloyd Detective Agency
Co-founder of the Christian Science / Invisible Science Church, Chicago, IL
A. B. A. Uranium Corp., 64 W. Randolph St., Chicago, 1 IL State of OK on Dec. 10, 1955, (1732 ½ NE 7th St., Oklahoma City, OK
Capital stock of $100,000 with $10.00 shares
Viasin Vitamins
Insurance
Funeral Home
Casket Co.
Hair Care – French Perm
WEAW Station – Sun. broadcast
Record Company
One of Founders of First Federal Savings and Loan
Law Firm with James Montgomery, Archie Weston in 1960
Senior Partner at the Law Firm Adams, Weston, Montgomery, Barnes, & Grant in 1940
Law Firm of Adams & Baker in 1923
Owner and Publisher of *The Enterprise Newspaper*
Publisher/Editor *Chicago World*

Vitae Charles Sumner Edwards II

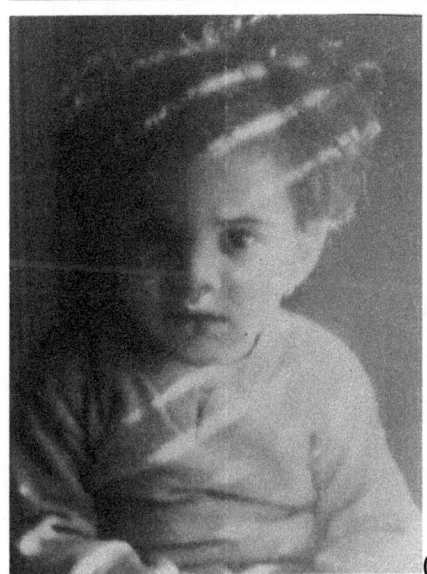
(Unk.)

Born:
September 26, 1921, in North Chicago, IL
to Charles S. and Katie (nee Schweigert) Edwards

Married:
September 8, 1948

Armed Services:
U. S. Army – Honorable Discharge 1941-1945

Education:
John Marshall Law School, 1946-1952
Roosevelt College, 1947-1948
Roosevelt University, 1972-1973, BS in Business Administration

Northeastern University, 1975–1976, MS in Urban Studies

Licenses/Trade Certifications:
Real Estate Broker's License, 1948-1953 & 1987 - 2001
Insurance Agent License, 1948
Notary Public, 1951
Journeyman Electrician
Radio, Radar, Maintenance and Repair
Electronics and Transmitter Theory
Code – Type
Engineering

Experience:
Electrician
    Griess-Phleger Tanning Co., 1939–1941 and 1946-1952
    Ford Motor Co., 1953-1956
    City of Chicago, 1956-1967
    Meade Electric Corp., 1968-1972
Licensed Real Estate Agent/Broker
    Habitat, 1994-1996
    Long & Foster, 1987–1994
    Illinois Realty (Broker & Owner), 1948-1953
Instructor in Electricity/Electronics, 1967–1985
    Southwestern University, Lake Michigan College, Triton College
    U. S. Navy & Royal Saudi Navy

Miscellaneous:
Rheem Mfg., 2/20/51 to 3/23/51
Checker Taxi, 7/2/52
Stewart-Warner, 9/15/52
Ford Motor, 12/1/53
King, Corliss, and Dunbar High Schools
Reporter - *Chicago World*
Republican Party Ward Committeeman

Awards:
IBEW Founder's Scholarship, 1975
Washington DC Board of Realtors' Distinguished Service Award

Volunteer Activities:
St. Thaddeus Fund Raising Committee (1962-69)
Realtor Institute Board of Governors (1994)
Public Policy Committee (1994)
Library and Convention Committees (1987-1989)
Education Committee (1989)
Residential Sales Council (1988-1993)
Residential Steering Committee (1993)
Mt. Pleasant Design, Historical Society, & Revolving Loan Committees (1988-89)
Calvary Shelter for Homeless Woman Board Member (1989-90)

Organizations:
International Fur & Leather Workers Union - President
International Brotherhood of Electrical Workers - Journeyman
MENSA
National Honor Society
Prometheans
Center Aisle Players

References

"2 Held To Jury for Taking Part in Cicero Riot," *Chicago Daily Tribune* (1923-1963); 30 October 1951; ProQuest Historical Newspapers Chicago Tribune (1849-1987), p. A2

"2 Timothy 4:7-8, *Holy Bible*, New Living Translation, 2nd ed., Tyndale House Publishing, Inc., 2004

"3 Cicero Cops Win New Trial in '51 Riot Case – Convictions of Chief, Two Aids Reversed," *Chicago Daily Tribune* (1923-1963); 10 March 1953; ProQuest Historical Newspapers Chicago Tribune (1849-1987), p. 3

"6 Testify That Cicero Leaders Fought Riot," *Chicago Daily Tribune* (1923-1963); 30 May 1952; ProQuest Historical Newspapers Chicago Tribune (1849-1987), p. A6

"500 Troops to Cicero!," *Chicago Daily Sun-Times*, 13 July, 1951, p. 1

"$4,300 Settlement OK'd in Cicero Riot Damage," *Chicago Daily Tribune* (1923-1963); 30 March 1957; ProQuest Historical Newspapers Chicago Tribune (1849-1987), p. 16

"4757 Grand Blvd. & 5138 S. Kenwood," *City of Chicago Tract & Plat Books*, Cook County Records Department, Books 347 and 355

"A Look at Cook County," http://alookatcook.com/1900/index.htm

Acheson, Harry, "The Woman Who Talks to the Dead," *Sepia Magazine*, June 1959, pp. 15-19

Adams, George C., "Lauds Barretts Course," *Chicago Daily Tribune* (1923-1963); 4 October 1941; ProQuest Historical Newspapers Chicago Tribune (1849-1987), p. 12

Adams, Geo. C., "Legal Hints," *The Chicago Whip*, 21 November, 1921

Adams, George C., "The People Speak," *Daily Defender* (Daily Ed.), 11 June 1956; ProQuest Historical Newspapers the Chicago Defender (1910-1975), p. 11

Adams, George C., Personal Notes & Statements (1948-71)

Adams, George C., "What the People Say, Atty George C. Adams," *The Chicago Defender*, (National ed., 1921-1967); 1 June 1935; ProQuest Historical Newspapers the Chicago Defender (1910-1975); p. 16

"Adams, George C.," *Who's Who in Colored America*: 6th ed., 1941/1944, by Thomas Yenser, publisher; "A biographical dictionary of notable living persons of Negro descent in America" (varies).

Adams, Minerva J., Personal Notes & Statements (1948-72)

"A Lesson in Heart," unknown

Anderson, David, "Cicero Urged to Seek God's Forgiveness," *Chicago Sun-Times*, 20 July 1951

"Arrest Cicero Riot Landlady on Southside," *Chicago Daily Tribune* (1923-1963); 29 December 1952; ProQuest Historical Newspapers Chicago Tribune (1849-1987), p. 2

"Avoid Cicero Riot Area, Chicagoans Warned," *The Chicago Sun-Times*: 15 July 1951, p. 4

Bilek, Art, *First Vice Lord: Big Jim Colosimo and the Ladies of the Levee*, Cumberland House Publishing, 2008

Blackwell, Lee, "Mob Scars Still Mar Riot Site," *The Chicago Defender*, (National ed., 1921-1967); 19 July 1952; ProQuest Historical Newspapers the Chicago Defender (1910-1975); p. 13

Bowman, Alice, Letter – Dec.1951

Boyle, John, Illinois States Attorney, "Illinois Grand Jury Transcript," Circuit Court of Cook County, 1951

"Bright's Disease," *Doctor's Treatment Website*, 2011, (http://www.doctortreatments.com

"Bright's Disease," *Medical Home Remedies, As Recommended by 19th and 20th Century Doctors*, http://www.doctortreatments.com/Chronic-Brights-Disease.html

Brinkerhoff, Clara W., "Letters to Charles S. Edwards," 6 February 1960 and 15 September 1960

"Building with Void Covenant Is Sold as a Co-op for Negroes," *The Chicago Tribune*: 18 November 1948, p.1, col. 3, early ed.

"Burnings," *The Daily News*: 12 July 1951, p.48

"Call National Guard to Quell Cicero Riot," *Chicago Daily News*, 12 July 1951, p. 1

"Central Figure in Cicero Riot Is War Veteran," *Chicago Daily Tribune* (1923-1963); 13 July 1951; ProQuest Historical Newspapers Chicago Tribune (1849-1987), p. 4

Chandler, Dean, Signed Illinois Realty (Southside Bank) checks to various people, 1951-1953

Chandler, Stella, Letter to Charles S. Edwards

Chepesiuk, Ron, *Black Gangsters of Chicago*, Barricade Books, 2007

Chicago Civil Liberties Committee, Civil Suit – "Action #510951" Filed on Behalf of Harvey E. and Johnetta Clark, Charles S. Edwards, Maurice Scott, Sr. and Jr. and Minerva J. Adams, 20 June 1951

"Chicago Guard to Cicero"

"Chicago Lawyer to Lead US Quiz on Cicero Riot," *Chicago Daily Tribune* (1923-1963); 6 October 1951; ProQuest Historical Newspapers Chicago Tribune (1849-1987), p. B9

"Cicero and American Justice," *The Chicago Defender*, (National ed., 1921-1967); 14 June 1952; ProQuest Historical Newspapers Chicago Defender (1910-1975); p. 10

"Cicero Area Pastors Sermonize on Riots"

"Cicero Bigots Made Happy," *The Chicago Defender*, (National ed., 1921-1967); 22 March 1952; ProQuest Historical Newspapers The Chicago Defender (1910-1975); p. 10

"Cicero Cop Told Him to 'Get Out,' Negro Attorney Testifies," *Chicago Daily Tribune* (1923-1963); 11 March 1952; ProQuest Historical Newspapers Chicago Tribune (1849-1987), p. 8

"Cicero Damage Amazes Jury"

"Cicero Erupts," *The Chicago Defender*: 21 July 1951

"Cicero Hoodlums Under Fire; War Vet, Family to Return", 21 July 1951, Unknown, vol. 1, no. 1

"Cicero Indictment Ruling Mon.," *Chicago Sun-Times*

"The Cicero Indictments," *The Chicago Sun-Times*: 14 December 1951

"Cicero – Phase II," *The Chicago Sun-Times*: 14 July 1951

"Cicero Police Failed Duty in Riot, Jury Told," *Chicago Daily Tribune* (1923-1963); 4 August 1951; ProQuest Historical Newspapers Chicago Tribune (1849-1987), p. 8

"The Cicero Riot," *Chicago Daily Tribune* (1923-1963); 14 July 1951; ProQuest Historical Newspapers Chicago Tribune (1849-1987), p. 8

"The Cicero Riot," *International Socialist Review*, ISR Issue 71, May–June 2010

"The Cicero Riot Story," *The Daily News*: 13 July 1951, p.28

"Cicero Riot Jury Winds Up Task in One Paragraf," *Chicago Daily Tribune* (1923-1963); 27 September 1951; ProQuest Historical Newspapers Chicago Tribune (1849-1987), p. C5

"Cicero Riot Sequel – Armed In Court, Landlady Jailed"

"Cicero," *Sundowner* Web Page, http://sundown.afro.illinois.edu/, 2011

"Cicero Riot Sequel – Armed in Court, Landlady Jailed," *The Chicago Herald*: 13 June 1952, p.1, vol. LII, #293 – PM

"Cicero Suits Deferred For US Jury Probe," *Chicago Daily Tribune* (1923-1963); 2 October 1951; ProQuest Historical Newspapers Chicago Tribune (1849-1987), p. 21

"City of Muskogee, OK," Muskogee Website, http://www.muskogeehistorian.com, 2011

"Clarks Ask $4,500 for Cicero Loss," *The Chicago Defender*, (National ed., 1921-1967); 19 July 1952; ProQuest Historical Newspapers The Chicago Defender (1910-1975); p. 1

Clark, Jr., Harvey, "Terror in Cicero," *Our World* Magazine, November 1951

"Clarks Will Not Quit Cicero Home," *The Chicago Defender*, (National ed., 1921-1967); 25 August 1951; ProQuest Historical Newspapers The Chicago Defender (1910-1975); p. 1

Cohen, Adam and Taylor, Elizabeth Little, *American Pharaoh: Mayor Richard J. Daley His Battle for Chicago and the Nation*, Brown and Co., 1st d., (May 2000)

Cofield, Ernestine, *The Chicago Defender*: 11 July 1962, p.8-9

Cofield, Ernestine, *The Chicago Defender*: 9 October 1962, "Cicero Would Riot Again To Bar Negro; Town Head," (p. 1, Daily ed.)

"Contracts," Freedman Bureau 163-1867, U. S. Archives

Cook County Records, "Marriage License of Charles S. Edwards to Catherine Schweigert," 8 June 1911

Cose, Ellis, *The Rage of a Privileged Class*, Harper and Collins, 1994

"Court Fines 10 and Frees 49 In Cicero Rioting," *Chicago Daily Tribune* (1923-1963); 6 October 1951; ProQuest Historical Newspapers Chicago Tribune (1849-1987), p. A5

"Creek Indians Seek $150,000,000 from US to Buy Defense Bonds," *The Chicago Defender,* (National ed., 1921-1967); 21 March 1942; ProQuest Historical Newspapers The Chicago Defender (1910-1975); p. 11

"Crowd Watches Family's Furniture Burn," *Chicago Daily News*, 12 July 1951, p.48

Cuomo, Sec. Andrew, "US v. Cicero," *HUD Archives*, 4 April 2000, HUD No. 00-70)

Curtis, Stephen R., John Marshall Law School, Letter: 12 March 1952

Curtis, Stephen R., John Marshall Law School, Letter: 23 July 1952

Davis, Clarice, *Chicago Sun-Times*, 8 November 1951

"Dawes Index," *National Archives*, U. S. Government

"Den License Is Gone," *Chicago Daily News*, 16 November 1903

De Rose, Camille, *The Camille De Rose Story* (1953) The De Rose Publishing Company, Chicago, IL

"Deutoronomy 11: 18-21," *Bible*, New Intertanational, 2010

District Court of the United States, "Civil Action Complaint #510951," June 20, 1951; The Northern District of Illinois, HARVEY

EVANS CLARK, JR., JOHNETTA CLARK, CHARLES EDWARDS, MAURICE SCOTT, JR., MAURICE SCOTT, SR., MINERVA J. ADAMS, Plaintiffs, v. HENRY J. SANDUSKY, individually and as President of he Town of Cicero, Ill.; JERRY JUSTIN, LEO KESPERSKY, JERRY DOLEZAL, JOHN KIMBARK, JOE CERNY, STANLEY PARA, JERRY HOLECEK, AND FRANK SPALE, individually and as Trustees of the Town of Cicero, Illinois; JERRY JUSTIN, individually and as Town Clerk of the Town of Cicero, Ill; Town of Cicero, a municipal corporation of the State of Illinois, Defendants

District Court of the United States, "Summons – Charles S. Edwards," 6 June 1951

Dorsey, James, "Master's Thesis," Unknown

Deuchler, Doug, "Cicero vs. Civil Rights," *The Town of Cicero Website*, http://www.thetownofcicero.com/, 9/26/2006

"Dr. Ephraim Ingals," *Chicago Medical Society Journal*, 1938

Edwards, Charles S., "Affidavit – Chicago Civil Liberties Committee," 10 June 1951; Notarized by Ira Latimer

Edwards, Charles S., Audio Interview for *StoryCorps*, 25 February, 2011, National Archives

Edwards, Charles S., "Audiotape Journals," 2006, 2008, 2009, 2010, 2011

Edwards, Charles S, "Autobiography," 1983

Edwards, Charles S., "Agreement with Clara W. Brinkerhoff," 7 April 1954

Edwards, Charles S., "Business Records," Illinois Realty, 1948-1952

Edwards, Charles S., "Letter to Brigadier General Milliken," Camp Crowder, MO, 22 June 1945

Edwards, Charles S., "Letter to Department of Registration and Education," Re: S. Chandler, 12 January 1953

Edwards, Charles S., "Letter to Dr. Seymour," Roosevelt University, 26 September 1972

Edwards, Charles S., "Letter to Hugo J. Kraslova & Co.," 25 May 1951

Edwards, Charles S., "Letter to International Fur and Leather Workers," 5 September 1942

Edwards, Charles S., "Letter to John Marshall Law School," 10 August 1951

Edwards, Charles S., "Letter to John Marshall Law School," 12 March 1952

Edwards, Charles S., Personal Notes, Records, & Statements (1948 to date)

Edwards, Charles S., Videotape Interview, 2011

Edwards, Charles S., "Sworn Affidavit to Chicago Civil Liberties Committee," 10 June 1951

"Expect Judge to Free 4 Today In Cicero Riot," *Chicago Daily Tribune* (1923-1963); 22 October 1951; ProQuest Historical Newspapers Chicago Tribune (1849-1987), p. 10

Fields, Margaret and Kerns, Jerome, "Pick Yourself Up," *Swing Time*, 1936

"Fines 3 Cops in Cicero Riot; Rips Landlady," *Chicago Daily Tribune* (1923-1963); 24 June 1952; ProQuest Historical Newspapers Chicago Tribune (1849-1987), p. 1

"First Witnesses Testify In US Cicero Riot Quiz," *Chicago Daily Tribune* (1923-1963); 6 November 1951; ProQuest Historical Newspapers *Chicago Tribune* (1849-1987), p. 12

"Fisk Grad Is Central Figure"

"Four Get $300 Each as Cicero Riot Suits End," *Chicago Daily Tribune* (1923-1963), 13 April 1957; ProQuest Historical Newspapers Chicago Tribune (1849-1987), p. 5

"French Creoles," (http://www.frenchcreoles.com), 2011

"From Riots to Renaissance: Bronzeville: The Black Metropolis," http://www.wttw.com, 2011

"Gets 2 Years, Tells Threat to Shoot Judge"

"Graft Men Defiant, Order Gaming Lid Off," *Chicago Daily News*, 21 October 1921

"Grand Boulevard," *Encyclopedia of Chicago*, (http://www.encyclopedia.chicagohistory.org/), 2011

"Grand Jury to Probe Cicero Outbursts," *The Chicago Defender*, (National ed., 1921-1967); 4 August 1951; ProQuest Historical Newspapers The Chicago Defender (1910-1975); p. 3

Haan, Dennis J., "Trouble," *Our Daily Bread*, 2 January 2011

"Halt Cicero Disorder," *Chicago Herald American*, 13 July 1951, p. 1

Hansen, H. Walter, "Real Estate Exam and License," State of Illinois, 3 August 1948

Hartford Boiler Inspection and Insurance, "Insurance Policy for Camille De Rose, 6319 19th St.," Assigned to La Salle National Bank Trust#13229, 5 May 1951

"Having Fun and Helping a Worthy Cause," *The Defender*, 18 June 1953, p. 26, "The Service League of Provident Hospital . . . Feminine pulchritude added glamour and beauty to occasion. Group included. [Mom]

Hayakawa, S. I., "Second Thoughts," *The Chicago Defender,* (National ed., 1921-1967); 23 June 1945; ProQuest Historical Newspapers The Chicago Defender (1910-1975); p. 13

Hill, Hazel C., "Letter to Charles S. Edwards," John Marshall Law School, 29 March 1949

Hirsch, Arnold, *Making the Second Ghetto – Race & Housing in Chicago, 1940-1960*, University of Chicago Press, 1998

Homer, Jack, "The Cicero Riots of 1951;" Chicago Commission Against Racial and Religious Discrimination, 22 July 1951, 2nd ed.

"How Mob Took Control Over Cicero," *The Chicago Sun-Times*: 13 July 1951

"How to Format a Manuscript for an EBook," http://workingwritersandbloggers.com, 2011

Ianni, Francis A. J., *Black Mafia*, Simon and Schuster, New York, 1974; p. 119

"Idlewild," *Lake County Website*, http://www.lakecountymichigan.com/idlewild.html

Illinois Realty, "Bills: Bureau of Water, Commonwealth Edison, Illinois Bell," 1951-1953

Illinois Realty, "Documents, Ads, Balance Sheets, Ledgers, Operating Statements, Real Estate Listings, Commissions," 1948-1953

"Insurance Receipt," Chandler's 1950 Pontiac DL Sedan, 12 December 1950

Jack, Homer A., "The Cicero Riots of 1951," The Council Against Racial and Religious Discrimination: 2nd ed.

Jackson, Elmer Carter & Gordon, Jacob U., *A Search for Equal Justice by African-American Lawyers: A History of the National Bar Association*, Authors Edition Illustrated, Vantage Press, 1999

Kara, John, "Letter to Illinois Realty," 19 September 1951

King Jr., Rev. Martin Luther, "How Long? Not Long," Chicago Leadership Council for Metropolitan Open Communities, Chicago, 1965

"La Promenade de Paris," *The Chicago Defender*, 28 June 1952, ProQuest Historical Newspapers The Chicago Defender (1910-1975), p. 6 – "Pleased with the success of the affair, which included a showing of the season's loveliest fashions are: [Mom], model"

Lake County, Michigan Website, http://www.lakecountymichigan.com, 2011

Lake County *News-Sun*, Waukegan, IL

Latimer, Ira, "Letter to Attorney General of the United States J. Howard McGrath," 11 June 1951

"Legal Notice to Drexel Forty-Four Corporation, A Suit Filed," Law Department of Cook County, 5 May 1951

"Lawyer Named By Grand Jury in Indictment, Lincoln State Bank," *The Chicago Defender*, (National ed., 30 July 1923; ProQuest Historical Newspapers The Chicago Defender (1910-1975), p. 2

Lee, Noble W., "Letter to Charles Edwards," The John Marshall Law School, 12 October 1951

Lee, Noble W., "Letter to Charles Edwards," The John Marshall Law School, 8 January 1952

Lee, Russell, "Negro Boys on Easter Sunday," Farm Security Administration/ Office of War Information, April 1941, Library of Congress

Lewy, Edward, "Letter to Charles S. Edwards," 17 August 1972

"Link Attorney to Ownership of Cicero Flats," *Chicago Daily Tribune* (1923-1963); 23 May 1952; ProQuest Historical Newspapers Chicago Tribune (1849-1987), p. 8

Loewen, James, *Lies My Teacher Told Me- Everything Your American Textbook Got Wrong*, Barnes & Noble Audio Book, 2003

Loewen, James, *Sundown Towns – A Hidden Dimension of American Racism*, Simon & Schuster, 2005

Lombardo, Robert, "The Black Mafia: African American Organized Crime in Chicago 1890-1960;" *Crime Law and Social Change* 38, pp 33-65, 2002, Kluwer Academic Publishers, Netherlands.

London and Lancashire Insurance, "Policy #C66594 on 6319 W. 19th," Payable to George C. Adams, 1 June 1951

Losonsley, Luther A., "Cicero Hoodlums Under Fire; War Vet, Family to Return," *The Chicago Enterprise*: 21 July 1951, p. 1 (Vol.1, #1)

Marshall Law School, John, "Transcript"

McCoo, Lucille and Jordis, "Letter to North American Accident Insurance Co.," 5 May 1952

McGill, Nathan, et al, "Family Photographs and Gelatin Silver Prints, 1910 to 1939," (Home 4806 South Parkway), Chicago Historical Society

"Measuring Worth," http://www.measuringworth.com/uscompare/, 2010

Meyer, Stephen Grant, *As Long As They Don't Move Next Door*, Rowman & Littlefield Publishers, Inc., 16 October 2001

"Mickey Finn – Drugs," Wikipedia Website, http://en.wikipedia.org/mickeyfinn-drugs, 2011

"Mobs and Law"

"NAACP Launches Defense Fund to Aid Clark Family," unknown

"Negroes Fix Curbs on Apts.," *The Chicago Sun-Times*: 19 November 1948, p.3, final ed.

Nicolaides, Becky and Wiese, Andrew, "Postwar Suburbs and the Construction of Race," *The Suburb Reader*, Rutledge Taylor Francis Group, 2006

"No More Ciceros!," NAACP Chicago Branch, 1951

"Notorious Chicago," http://chicagology.com/notorious-chicago

"Officials Rap Slum Conditions – Families Herded Into 'Black Belt,'" *The Chicago Defender*, (National ed., 1921-1967); 31 August 1936; ProQuest Historical Newspapers The Chicago Defender (1910-1975); p. 3

"Opinion of the People"

"Opposed Negro Lease, Cicero Officials Say," *Chicago Daily Tribune* (1923-1963); 29 August 1951; ProQuest Historical Newspapers Chicago Tribune (1849-1987), p. 2

"Our Opinions – How Much Is Freedom Worth," *The Chicago Defender*, (National ed., 1921-1967); 12 March 1955; ProQuest Historical Newspapers The Chicago Defender (1910-1975); p. 9

"Our Opinions – No One to Blame," *The Chicago Defender*, (National ed., 1921-1967); 11 December 1954; ProQuest Historical Newspapers The Chicago Defender (1910-1975); p. 9

"Owner of Cicero Riot Building In Court Today," *Chicago Daily Tribune* (1923-1963); 23 June 1952; ProQuest Historical Newspapers Chicago Tribune (1849-1987), p. A4

"Notable Kentucky African Americans Database," *University of Kentucky*, http://www.uky.edu/Libraries/NKAA/, 2011

Peter 1:4, *Bible*, New Intertanational, 2010

Pflaum, Irving, "Expediency and Cicero"

"Policy Players Win on 4-1-44," *Chicago Tribune*, 5 February 1898.

"Policy Sam," Illinois Writers Project, Box 35, #18, *Negro in Illinois*, Woodson Library, Chicago, IL

"'Policy' Sam Held Up," *Chicago Defender*, 22 December 1928, p. 5

"'Policy' Sam Young Rites Held Friday," *Chicago Defender*, 22 May 1937

Powell, Cader, "Will of Cader Powell – June 4, 1830," Probate: State of North Carolina Hertford County, Court of Pleas, Feb. 1831

"Private Detective License – George C. Adams," State of Illinois, Department of Registration and Education, 19 March 1957

'Proverbs 3: 1-35," *Holy Bible*, Tyndale Publishing Co., 2004, New Living Translation, 2nd ed.

"Race Group Hits Indictment of 6 In Cicero Riots," *Chicago Daily Tribune* (1923-1963); 20 September 1951; ProQuest Historical Newspapers Chicago Tribune (1849-1987), p. B11

"Real Estate Broker" License, State of Illinois, 17 June 1948

Redel, H. S., "Notice of Chattel Mortgage," Cook County, ILL., 1 July 1952

"Riot Jury Told of Dual Role of An Agitator," *Chicago Daily Tribune* (1923-1963); 15 August 1951; ProQuest Historical Newspapers Chicago Tribune (1849-1987), p. 20

"Riots in Cicero Linked to Move to Sell Building," *The Chicago Tribune*: 19 October 1951, p.14

"Riot Indictment Bares Woman's Police Record," *Chicago Daily Tribune* (1923-1963); 22 September 1951; ProQuest Historical Newspapers Chicago Tribune (1849-1987), p. 6

"Sheriff Checks Mob Threat as Family Enters Apt.," Pittsburgh, PA, 14 July 1951

"Sites Near Union Station," http://www.dhke.com/CRJ/station.html

"Six Indicted In Cicero Riot," *Chicago Daily Tribune* (1923-1963); 19 September 1951; ProQuest Historical Newspapers Chicago Tribune (1849-1987), p. 1

Skultety, John, "Workmen's Compensation Insurance," 5 June 1950 and 15 September 1950

"Slate 80th Birthday Fete For Rev. Adams," *The Chicago Daily Defender*, (Daily Edition, 1960-1973); 29 June 1964; ProQuest Historical Newspapers The Chicago Defender (1910-1975), p. 6

Sonderby, Max, "Cicero Riot Probers to Hear Judge's Order," Unknown

Spear, Allan, *Black Chicago*, Chicago: University of Chicago, 1967; p. 76

"Stench Bombing of Berwyn House Echoes Vets Troubles in Cicero"

"Sues 12 for $1,000,000 Over 1951 Cicero Riot"

"Sues for Title To Building In Cicero Rioting," *Chicago Daily Tribune* (1923-1963); 18 August 1951; ProQuest Historical Newspapers Chicago Tribune (1849-1987), p. A8

Sugrue, Thomas J. *Sweet Land of Liberty: The Forgotten Struggle for Civil Rights in the North*, Random House, Hardcopy, 2008, 1st ed., p. 228

Sus, Audrey, "Letter from John Marshall Law School to Charles Edwards," 2 August 1951

"Telephone Co. Sued By Atty. George Adams – Claims City is Owed Over $15,000,000," The *Chicago Daily Defender*, (National Edition, 1921-1967); 2 April 1932; ProQuest Historical Newspapers The Chicago Defender (1910-1975), p. 4

"Tells of Cicero Threat to Dr."

"Tells Threats by Flat Owner in Riot Trial," *Chicago Daily Tribune* (1923-1963); 29 May 1952; ProQuest Historical Newspapers Chicago Tribune (1849-1987), p. 4

Tennessee State Records, Marriage of Frank Lampton to Susan Campbell, 18 April, 1866

Thompson, Nathan, *Kings - The True Story of Chicago's Policy Kings and Numbers Racketeers*, The Bronzeville Press, 2006

Towndey, Luther A., "Veteran Moves into Cicero This Week," *The Chicago Defender*: 7 July 1941 (Error on paper – should be 1951)

"Train Stations & Railroads," http://www.dhke.com/CRJ/station.html)

Travis, Dempsey J., *An Autobiography of Black Chicago*, Urban Research Press, 1991

"Troops Halt Cicero Disorder," *Kansas City Herald American*: 13 July 1951

"Troops Jail 157 Hoodlums," *The Chicago Defender*: 21 July 1951

Unknown, *The Pittsburgh Courier*

"U. S. Census," U. S. Government, 1850-1930

"U. S. Jury Probe of Cicero Riot Reported Over" *Chicago Daily Tribune* (1923-1963); 7 December 1951; ProQuest Historical Newspapers Chicago Tribune (1849-1987), p. 16

"U. S. Maps Cicero Riot Quiz," *Chicago Daily Tribune* (1923-1963); 28 September 1951; ProQuest Historical Newspapers Chicago Tribune (1849-1987), p. 1

"U. S. Supreme Court Ruling, Hansberry v. Lee, 311 U.S. 32 (1940), 311 U.S. 32, HANSBERRY et al. v. LEE et al., No. 29. ;" Argued, 25 October 1940, Decided 12 November 1940.; *Case Law Website*, http://caselaw.lp.findlaw.com, 2011

"U.S. Supreme Court Ruling, Shelley v. Kraemer, 334 U.S. 1 (1948), 334 u.s. 1, Shelley et ux. v. Kraemer et ux. McGhee et ux. v. Sipes et al., nos. 72, 87;" argued 15, 16 January 1948; decided 3 May 1948; [Shelley v. Kraemer 334 u.s. 1 (1948)] [334u.s. 1, 2], *Case Law Website*, http://caselaw.lp.findlaw.com, 2011

"United States Court of Appeals Seventh Circuit Decision, (243 F.2d 705), Joseph BEAUHARNAIS, Plaintiff-Appellant, v. The PITTSBURGH COURIER PUBLISHING CO., Inc., Defendant-Appellee, No. 11670," 19 April 1957.Rehearing denied 10 May 1957, *Justia Website*, http://supreme.justia.com/

"United States 7th Circuit Court of Appeals Reports, Clark v. Sandusky, 205 F.2d 915 (7th Cir. 1953), No. 10846," *Courts Website*, 20 July 1953 http://bulk.resource.org/courts.gov, 2011

Upsham, Mrs., "Letter to George C. Adams, Attorney," 13 July 1951

Walker, Lewis and Wilson, Ben, *The Idlewild Community – Black Eden*, Michigan State University Press, 2002

"Warrant - Charles S. Edwards," U. S. Marshall's Office, 1951

"What Kind of People Make A Mob? Cicero Rioters Are A Varied Group," *The Enterprise*

White, Walter, *The Crisis*, October 1919

Wilkerson, Isabel, *The Warmth of Other Suns – The Epic Story of America's Great Migration*, Random House, 2010

Wolf, Sherry, *ISR Issue* 71, May–June 2010, Review of The fight for civil rights up North – Review of Sugrue's Book – *Sweet Land of Liberty*, http://www.isreview.org/issues/71/rev-sugrue.shtml

"Woman Owner Charges Cicero Plot to Lawyer," *Chicago Daily Tribune* (1923-1963); 14 March 1952; ProQuest Historical Newspapers Chicago Tribune (1849-1987), p. 13

Young, Jewell, Personal Letters, Notes, & Statements (1948 to 1991)

Young, [Mom], Personal Letters (1951-1953)

Young, Ralph, Winston, Lind, and Young, "Letter to Charles Edwards, Edwards v. South Side Bank & Trust Co.," 31 March 1957

Photographs

Adams, George C., "Cicero Crowds, " 1951

Adams, George C., "Cicero Crowds Day of Move," 1951

Adams, George C., "Cicero Crowds Before Riot," July 1951

Adams, George C., "Jewell in France," 1951

Adams, Minerva, "Parties Meet in Courthouse" – George C. Adams, Anthony Berkos, Joe Clayton, Harvey & Johnetta Clark, Charles S. Edwards, Ed Konovsky, George Leighton, Thurgood Marshall, Maurice Scott, Jr., Unknown

Edwards, Charles S., "4 Shots Fired Through Window," 1951

Edwards, Charles S., "6319 W. 19th, Cicero," May 1951

Edwards, Charles S., "6319 W. 19th, Cicero Building Damage," July 1951

Edwards, Charles S., "Officers and Cicero Building Damage2," July 1951

Edwards, Charles S., "Illinois Realty's listing photo for the Walgreen Mansion, " 1949

Edwards, Lucille Y., "Can You Identify Him? Stand up!," 1952 Drawing

Unknown:
"Atty. George C. Adams outside his law office in downtown Chicago, 1951"

"Charles Sumner Edwards II, 1925"

"Charles Sumner Edwards II, 1951"

"George C. Adams, 1921"

"National Guardsmen and rioters during the Cicero Riot, July 1951"

National Guardsmen and rioters during the Cicero Riot, July 1951 (unk.)

Necrology

Susan Campbell (1807), Randall Bradshaw, Lucinda Campbell Lampton (1842-1915), Frank Campbell, Ambrose Morrison (1790), Delilah Lampton (1800), Frank Lampton (1823-1923), Albert Lampton (1819), Howard Lampton (1820), Minerva Lampton Banks (1824), Lewis Banks, Edward Payne, Maria Wallace (1850), Lyman Wallace (1845), Emma Wallace (1869), Lewis Wallace (1870), Mary Jane Lampton (1825), Minerva Lampton Young Adams (1875-1972), Samuel Young (1872-1902), Sam Young (1847), Amanda Young (1854), George Powell (1690-1736), Cader Powell (1715-1771), Lewis Powell (1743-1778), Cader Powell (1771-1830), Jesse R. Powell (1819), Washington Powell (1825), Rachel Powell (1830), Alice Powell Hubbard (1852-1919), Luis Hubbard (1849), Della Powell (1867), Courtney Powell Cage Pickett Armstrong (1870-1951), Margaret Cage (1868), Henry Bowman (1845), Mary Bowman (1880), Helen Bowman (1882), Susan Bowman (1883), Garfield Bowman (1886), Robert Bowman (1887), Kenneth Bowman (1891), Henry Bowman (1896), Ida (1864), Sade, Wave Beatty (1889), Alice, Molly Lampton (1858), Mary Lampton (1858), Ora Lampton, Lillian Lampton, Albert Lampton (1863), Sue Lampton Perkins (1878-1920), Louis Perkins, Henry Cage, Alice Cage (1891), Azzalee Cage (1884), Hernanda Cage (1887-1965), William Cage, Calie Cage (1888), Reginald Cage, Aunt Cora, Uncle Monte, Maude Carter, George Cage, Virgil Cage, Albert "A.P." Cage, William Powell (1888), Robert Hubbard (1843), Henry Davis (1845), Charles Adams (1860), Mr. Stious, Violet Gibson Adams (1858-1944), George Adams (1884-1971), Charles Edwards I (1880–1947), John Schweigert (1824-1905), Rosanna Schweigert (1826), William Schweigert (1855-1939), Catherine Schweigert Edwards (1895–1945), Charity Edwards (1911-1912), Charles R. Edwards (1816), Margaret Patterson Edwards (1818), Jesse Edwards, Joshua Edwards, Andrew, Mary Edwards, Harry Robinson, Austin Edwards, Joseph Edwards, Hank Edwards (1875), William H. Patterson (1878–1923), Andrew Harrison (1830), Carey Ann Harrison (1840), Margaret Harrison (1800), Versie Harrison Garner (1873-1929), Taylor Garner (1855), Rosa Harrison Watson (1898), Mattie Harrison Carroll (1899), John Carroll (1900), Jim Watson

(1895), James Watson (1920), Catherine Watson (1921), Linda Harrison (1868), Amelia Harrison (1870), Mack Harrison (1877), Fannie Harrison Evans (1880), Owen Evans, Oscar "O. C." Evans, Lewis Evans, Fifton Evans, Agnes Evans, Baxter Evans, Bea Jackson Sales, Mr. Sales, Zeffa Jackson Dickelson, Van Kermit Dickelson (1904-1963), James Thompson (1873), Mattie Harrison Thompson (1875–1943), Mr. Armstrong, Lucille Armstrong Young (1905 - 1953), Siegel Young Sr. (1900–1989), Nathaniel Adler, Sr. (1923–1988), George Young (1928–1965), Jewell Young (1924-1991), Vivian Young Adler (1926–2009), Kenneth Vallis (1930-1997), Nathaniel Adler Jr. (1956–2000), Georges Benjamin (1928–2005), Tessie Edwards Benjamin (1919–2008), John Benjamin (1960–1976), Tony Young, Bette Holeman Young (1931–2008), Wesley McGuthry, Jean Noah (1935-2004), Joseph W. Poole, Jr. (1914), Archie Watkins (1906–1986), Roosevelt Bridges, Malinda Thompson Bridges, John Thompson, Sarah Thompson, Mrs. Patterson, Susan Scott (1922), Bennie Carroll (1936-1988), Geneva Carroll Wright (1925), Elizabeth Carroll (1927), Rosa Etta Carroll, Estelle Carroll, Margie Carroll, Mattie Lue Carroll, Oscar Carroll (1929), James Carroll (1924), John Carroll (1924), and all the unknown family. . .

About H. M. Edwards:

H. M., born and raised in Chicago, has been a professional tennis player and coach, college tennis coach, and certified teaching tennis professional for the past forty years. She has advanced degrees and certification in Corrections-Psychology and a degree in Aviation.

Also by H. M. Edwards:

"A Love For All Seasons" - *America*

"All Right, I Guess" - *The Light of The World*

BLT - Basketball, Love, and Tennis

Could It Be Your Neighbor

The Psychopathology of Personality Disorders

The Secret of Doubles

www.ingramcontent.com/pod-product-compliance
Lightning Source LLC
Chambersburg PA
CBHW071456040426
42444CB00008B/1366